Grietas

A Journal of Zapatista Thought and Horizons

Issue 1   Spring/Summer 2022
Autonomy from Below and to the Left in the U.S.

Sexta Grietas del Norte Editorial Committee
Jared Cetz
Enrique Davalos
Yaneth Escobosa
Gustavo Garcia
Maritza Geronimo
Roberto D. Hernández
Vaughn Love
Ymoat Luna
Caitlin Manning
Kristian E. Vasquez

Web
www.sextagrietasdelnorte.org

Email
journal@sextagrietasdelnorte.org

Social Media
@sextagrietasdelnorte (IG) @sextagrietas (Twitter)

Introducing *Grietas:*
A Journal of Zapatista Thought and Horizons

Sexta Grietas del Norte Editorial Committee

Grietas: cracks in the walls of power, fissures in the capitalist monoculture, faultines in the hierarchies of hetero-patriarchal, class, and racial oppression. We fight the obsessive individualism, the relentless economic logic, the cruel and extractive exploitation of the natural world that destroys everything in its path.

Grietas: A Journal of Zapatista Thought and Horizons seeks to accompany and celebrate the resistances and rebellions that emerge from the outside and in-between spaces where other worlds persist and new ones are built and envisioned; where paths to autonomy and communal ways of life are forged; where capitalist destruction of nature is resisted; where Zapatista and decolonial horizons are enacted. This journal is a space to share theory, analysis, thoughts, feelings, and experiences of what we tentatively call "autonomy" from the civilization of death, with its entangled hierarchies of domination that have marked the modern/colonial world over the long night of 530 years.

From our vantage point, there is no question that the storm the Zapatistas warned us of has arrived: climate catastrophe, the Covid-19 pandemic, the never-ending pursuit of new frontiers of capitalist extraction and commodification (be it on earth, in outer space, or cyberspace), insurgent far-right and fascist movements, the intensifying dispossession and exploitation of those from below by those from above. In these uncertain and tumultuous times, when those in power have nothing to offer other than maintaining the rapacious capitalist status quo, we who struggle from below and to the left organize to transform our conditions and to create and defend other worlds we know are possible because they already exist.

This journal is a contribution to resistance and rebellion, and an homage to the principles, practices, and visions of the Zapatista peoples, the Zapatista National Liberation Army (EZLN), and Mexico's National Indigenous Congress (CNI) and its Indigenous Governing Council (CIG), which are more important than ever as we struggle for life and dignity in our geographies north of the wall. While we expect that many who pick up this journal are familiar with the EZLN's uprising and struggle for autonomy, we recognize that many within our geographies don't have the same understanding of the CNI-CIG, and it excites us to introduce readers to their struggles and visions.

For its part, the National Indigenous Congress (CNI), a sister organization of the EZLN, was constituted on October 12, 1996 as "the home of the Indigenous peoples... a space where originary peoples can find shared thought and solidarity to strengthen their struggles of resistance and rebellion, with their own forms of organization, representation, and decision-making."[1] The CNI say their founding peoples inherit five centuries "of extermination, violence, domination, and plunder from capitalism and its allies, the owners of power and money, the representatives of death."[2] As they put it, "We do not forget. Because that blood, that history, those lives, those struggles are the essence of our resistance and our rebellion that turns into autonomy, ancestral

---

1 "What Is the CNI?" http://www.congresonacionalindigena.org/what-is-the-cni
2 "What Is the CNI?"

revendications of education, security, justice, spirituality, communication, self-defense, and self-government."[3]

The peoples that make up the CNI organize by following seven principles of *mandar obedeciendo* (leading by obeying), where who is obeyed is the assembly, not the leadership. Our network, Sexta Grietas del Norte, organizes by these principles as well:

Serve, don't serve yourself
Represent, don't replace
Build, don't destroy
Obey, don't command
Propose, don't impose
Convince, don't defeat
Go below, don't go above

When the Zapatistas published the *Sixth Declaration of the Lacandon Jungle* in 2005, the CNI became an adherent to its invitation that all of us across Planet Earth struggle together from below, for the below, and against capital, remaining steadfast in our insistence that another world is possible, a world where difference is respected, a world were many worlds fit.

Two decades after its founding, the CNI would create the Indigenous Governing Council (CIG), a political body formed by 523 communities of 43 indigenous peoples of Mexico, each community with one councilman and one councilwoman elected in assemblies by *usos y costumbres* (traditions and customs). The CIG made the decision to present their spokesperson, María de Jesús Patricio Martínez, better known as Marichuy, as a candidate in Mexico's presidential elections in an attempt to derail the paid media's electoral spotlight on the politics of the above. From the beginning, the CIG stated that the purpose of their electoral campaign was neither to win the elections nor to take power. They directed their message to "original peoples and civil society" in the hopes of amplifying their call to organize in order to stop the destruction of the country, strengthen resistance and rebellion, and defend "the life of each person,

3 "What Is the CNI?"

every family, collective, community, or neighborhood."[4] The CIG is defined as "the collective word from below and to the left, that shakes the world when the earth trembles with epicenters of dignity and autonomy."[5] The CIG is understood as the form of organization "in which peoples organize ourselves to take decisions about the issues and problems that involve all of us. It is the other form of doing politics, horizontally, from collective analysis, and decision-making."[6] The CIG, together with the CNI and the EZLN, constitute a powerful force of Indigenous peoples resisting the torrent of capitalist mega-investments that destroy nature and tear apart the social fabric in Mexico as in the rest of the world.

In this issue's first section, "Autonomy from Below and to the Left in the U.S." is explored from a variety of perspectives, each contribution reflecting on past and current struggles for liberation, while offering glimpses of possible autonomous futures inspired by Zapatismo and the seven principles of leading by obeying. On the definition of "autonomy," we do not attempt to provide a definitive answer or a universal definition and instead offer a collage of reflections from our network of U.S.-based adherents to the *Sixth*, Sexta Grietas del Norte, as well as essays, poetry, and speculative fiction. In this first section, you will also encounter a candid talk by a veteran of the Black Panther Party and Black Liberation Army and former political prisoner Ashanti Alston on his discovery of Zapatismo, where he reflects on the similarities and differences between the Zapatista struggle for autonomy and the Black Panther Party and Black Liberation Army. We invite you to continue this collective process of *caminando preguntando* (asking questions while walking) as we figure out how to navigate this storm, how to resist it, and how we might build with one another.

In the next section, "Reportbacks," Grietas members offer testimonies of projects we've accompanied the Zapatistas and the CNI-CIG on, including the Zapatistas' march on Madrid on August 13, 2021; encounters

4 "May the Earth Tremble at Its Core" https://enlacezapatista.ezln.org.mx/2016/10/18/may-the-earth-tremble-at-its-core. Also see: "A Story to Try to Understand" https://enlacezapatista.ezln.org.mx/2016/11/26/a-story-to-try-to-understand

5 "Indigenous Governing Council" http://www.congresonacionalindigena.org/indigenous-governing-council

6 "Indigenous Governing Council"

with food as medicine in Zapatista autonomous communities; and an Autonomous Health Brigade supporting an embattled CNI community set up an autonomous health clinic.

In the third and final section, "Zapatista Praxis," you will find an in-depth chronology of the first leg of the "Journey for Life of the EZLN and CNI," which took place in Europe in 2021. It includes insights on the meanings and understandings that evolved over journey's path. The Zapatista intention of listening and learning is noted in their journey and echoed and developed in the contribution, "Zapatista Seed Pedagogics," a Zapatista-inspired form of collective teaching, learning, and building. We also include a transcribed interview with Rosaluz Perez, who spent almost decade in the Zapatista communities, from whom we learn about the critical role of women in Zapatista autonomy.

Grietas: A Journal of Zapatista Thought and Horizons is our offering of respect, solidarity, and encounter to those taking paths towards autonomy and away from the capitalist hydra, each from our own geographies, with our own calendars, in our own ways. The considerable work involved in producing these pages was a labor of love: only the printers were paid. We hope to get to know you and your paths, and we invite you to engage with us and one another.

Contributors

Ashanti Alston is a father, an anarchist, a prison abolitionist, and a former member of the Black Panther Party and Black Liberation Army. He was a political prisoner for over a decade and continues to work with the Jericho Movement to free all political prisoners.

Rosa María Barajas is Chilanga/fronteriza from Purepecha roots. Independent communicator, who accompanies and visualizes struggles of Peoples and movements that fight for life and defend Mother Earth. Her heart and convictions are with Zapatismo. Part of Raíces sin Fronteras (borderland Tijuana San Diego) and Grietas en el Muro (Mexico City).

Enrique Davalos is MeXicano, Marxista, Zapatista, history profe who honors Freire and collaborates with Raíces sin Fronteras (borderland Tijuana San Diego) and Grietas en el Muro (Mexico City).

Gustavo García is a member of Chicanx World Making and Futurities Project and Cafe y Rebeldia. He is a PhD student in Chicana/o Studies at the University of New Mexico, Pueblo lands.

Roberto D. Hernández is a member of Xican@patistas Autonomxs, Autonomia Xochitequio, the Centro Cultural de la Raza, and a profe of Chicana/o Studies at SDSU in unceded Kumeyaay territory.

Gisselle Jiménez, **Jess Kulig**, **Corbin Laedlein**, and **Michelle Yun** are participants in the Sunset Park Popular Assembly, an autonomous space for organizing, decision making, and community building that was launched in 2019 in Sunset Park, Brooklyn.

Ymoat Luna is a writer with Xican@patistas Autonomxs, cultural worker, and activist currently part of Centro Cultural de la Raza, Detention Resistance, and Autonomia Xochitequio in the borderlands of unceded Kumeyaay peoples, San Diego, California.

Caitlin Manning is an anticapitalist feminist based in a four generation household in San Francisco. They make films, write, translate and organize with like minded rebels and resistors. Member of Chiapas Support Committee, Oakland, Ca.

Rosaluz Perez is a feminist sociologist. She belongs to the generation of young people who, beginning in 1994, were formed by accompanying the struggle of the Zapatista communities. She has just completed a doctorate that presents an analysis of the fundamental role that women have had in the conception and construction of Zapatista autonomy.

Charlotte María Sáenz is a community artist and scholar currently developing a Seed Pedagogics praxis that accompanies Zapatismo and other liberation struggles. As part of The Deep Medicine Circle in the Ohlone territories of the Raymatush and Chochenyo peoples, they work on decolonizing land, food, medicine, stories, learning, and restoration.

Natalia M. Toscano is a member of Chicanx World Making and Futurities Project and Cafe y Rebeldia. She is a PhD student in Chicana/o Studies at the University of New Mexico, located in unceded Pueblo lands.

Kristian E. Vasquez is a Xicano writer, zinester, and facilitator with Eagle and Condor Liberation Front, Chicanx World Making and Futurities Project, and Wild Seed. He is also a PhD student in the Department of Chicana and Chicano Studies at UC Santa Barbara, located on the unceded lands of Anisq'oyo, Chumash territories.

What Does Autonomy Mean to You?

Members of Sexta Grietas del Norte

*   *   *

from the Eagle and the Condor Liberation Front

Autonomy is the practice of collective freedom that desires a commitment to a praxis of struggle for another world in motion. Autonomy allows for the creation of spaces (not necessarily physical) within already existing worlds. These spaces give room to collectively grow, learn, unlearn, and exist with each other not against each other. Autonomy for us is a practice against oppression, and in the case of our context, is anti-capitalist and anti-colonial.

Autonomy is knowing we have the power to control our own body, community, economies, and land through the ways we see fit to meet our needs. We do not need to restrict ourselves to state-imposed definitions or regulations, moving beyond this creating our own worlds even while white settler colonialism/coloniality/and capitalist institutions still exist. Autonomy is a praxis.

—Los Angeles, California

* * *

from Charlotte

Autonomy, as inspired by Zapatismo, is an ongoing, daily process of collectively building a dignified life for all. It is built by creating and reintegrating systems of and for life: for example, in agroecology, self-government, economics, education, justice, health, arts, and sciences... all responding to the evolving needs of our communities, human and beyond-human.

Autonomy builds on the ancestral Indigenous wisdom of our diverse peoples in order to recreate better ways of being in relationship with one another. This construction needs to include the participation of all, so that collective action can reflect collective voice while respecting the self-determination of each. The collective does not supplant the brilliance of each person; on the contrary, each contribution nourishes the common good. This is how we can build autonomous community in our places that respects all of life.

—Territory of Huichin and Jovel (a.k.a. Oakland and SCLC)

* * *

from Semillas

When thinking about what we mean by autonomy, the topic of time comes up a lot: autonomy connects to the privilege of having access to time and being able to choose what you do with your time. Self-determination also comes up for us as being able to choose how we want to live and having our own materials/resources as a means of production without the need to depend on any institution, government, or corporation.

We agree that land is vital in order to have autonomy. Land that belongs to the community and is a safe space to exist, convivir, to commune, organize, grow food, create, and heal. What makes it safe? Some of us express it as a space needed for "community only." Others among us argue that it should be a designated space only for People of Color (POC). This has led us into a bigger discussion on "who/what is community?" and how do we create "a world where many worlds may fit?" This has also led us into a broader conversation around decolonization, gentrification, neo-colonization, and the idea of the lines that have been drawn to divide us globally, and whether "true autonomy" can only be achieved if we return to our native lands or to the neighborhoods where we were born and grew up in. We all agree that a safe space is a place where *el estado*, or the state, cannot enter or have any power over the land or the community in that space. Autonomy to many of us also means being able to have the most basic human rights like education and health without depending on money and without having to undergo any kind of "evaluation" from el estado and its institutions to determine if we meet the criteria to deserve rights such as health care, housing, and education.

On how we practice autonomy, as a collective we try our best to create spaces to heal and build with our communities. We are proud of the many social justice films and art projects we have realized and produced with the community without depending on any institution. NYC is extremely expensive, and through collaboration and sharing of resources, many times we have been able to accomplish the impossible. Still, we realize that many of the spaces that we've created have been on land/space that never belongs to the community; it's almost like we float to different sites, and so the idea of whether or not it's possible for a space to be "autonomous" and "safe" temporarily makes us wonder: can it float, can it transform to adapt to the realities and challenges that expensive cities/urban spaces present? Is it a "state of mind" or a verb, not just some metaphor? We must continue to reimagine autonomy and not be afraid to transform spaces, the way the EZLN teaches us. In sharing what we think about autonomy, we are left with more questions than answers, but we hope that this summary can contribute to conversations on how we understand and can practice this and grow autonomy in the belly of the capitalist beast.

—New York City, New York

* * *

from Raíces sin Fronteras

Discussing autonomy brings up important memories and concepts such as "councils," "communes," "duality of power," "germs of popular power," etc. These concepts condense important past and present experiences that focused, on the one hand, on the destruction of capitalist domination, and, on the other hand, on the creation or recreation of community life with principles and values opposed to capitalism. Many perspectives have inspired these historical struggles, for example, those of the socialists, communists, and anarchists. Our thinking-feeling is that the Zapatista experience offers a perspective that values, weighs, and breaks down but yet continues those perspectives; it is thus an effort not to deny them, but to incorporate them dialectically, and it does so on the basis of recovering organizational forms of native peoples, such as community assemblies. For us, all of this goes hand in hand with autonomy.

The Zapatista perspective for autonomy is anti-capitalist and carries a simultaneous yes and a no. Neo-Zapatismo recognizes the great socialist and communist debates and battles of the 19th century and the beginning of the 20th. However, neo-Zapatismo is above all, a seed that sprouts in the times of neoliberal capitalism and in lands and peoples "from below" of one of the most excluded territories of the Global South: Chiapas. The neo-Zapatista movement is not incidental; it is one of the most notable and successful expressions of the struggles, rebellions, and resistance that neoliberal capitalism, or the Fourth World War, as the Zapatistas call it, inevitably engenders. This Indigenous movement calls us to fight for autonomy with "rebellion" and "resistance."

For the Zapatistas, "rebellion" means NO! to the system. It is the struggle to destroy the capitalist hydra, to tear and deepen cracks in its walls. At the same time, "resistance" means YES! to something else that is possible. It is the effort to start building another world from now on, at the same time that the present world is being destroyed ("The Crack in the Wall. First Note on Zapatista Method," *Enlace Zapatista*, May 2015). The Zapatistas put them together because their tactic simultaneously considers rebellion and resistance, a NO! and a YES!, unlike some Marxist-Leninist proposals that focus on the NO! and relegate or postpone any practical consideration of the YES! to a future after the overthrow of the capitalist state. It is not like those who seek a YES! within the system, for example taking over governments or creating cooperatives that just adapt to the neoliberal market, or organizing collectives that create bubbles trying to escape separately from capitalism, but without proposing the common struggle to destroy it for everyone.

The Zapatista experience inspires us, therefore, to fight for life and against death in our own geographies, calendars, and in our own ways. It inspires us to open and deepen "cracks" against the capitalist hydra, which on its path despoils and attempts to annihilate anything and anyone that it finds not useful for itself; cracks such as those opened by peoples protesting gas pipelines, migrants marching against borders, movements against police brutality and racism, struggles for abolition, or workers striking against labor exploitation. The networks in solidarity, for example, with the struggles of the National Indigenous Congress, are also cracks in the walls of capitalism.

For life, building "resistances" in our territories means cultivating seeds of alternative and anti-capitalist civilizations and generating another education, another way of production with egalitarian labor relationships, another health, another culture, and another form of community relationship that celebrates differences, embraces coincidences, and refuses to reproduce the existing hierarchical and patriarchal system.

For life, it means weaving resistances based on another feeling-thinking where consumerism is questioned and respect for Mother Earth prevails; resistances that are neither mirrors nor identical, but that embrace each other in rebellion to mow down the capitalist hydra's weeds. As SupGaleano put it in a June 2021 communique entitled, "The Journey for Life: To What End?":

> Each person, according to their calendar, their geography, and their customs, will have to make their path, and just like us Zapatista peoples, they will stumble and get up, and what they build will have whatever name they want to give it.

The Zapatista perspective invites us, then, to fight for a world in which many worlds fit, where everything is for everyone, nothing just for ourselves, and where whoever rules, leads by obeying. These simple yet profound principles guide our efforts for freedom, justice, peace, and democracy, and against exploitation, plunder, repression, and contempt. In short, for life, and against death. This is how we understand the Zapatista perspective on the struggle for autonomy.

—Mexico City and San Diego

* * *

from Gustavo

Autonomy is a collective and collaborative process where people work together to fight against oppression, violence, dehumanization, and hierarchies while also implementing another form of relating to one another and existing.

Autonomy is a shared responsibility where everyone participates and gives back to the people, land, and community in whatever way, shape or form.

Autonomy as a process to collective living and a practice of shared responsibilities that ensure the survivability and well being of a people and community.

Autonomy is the practice of creating and sustaining communal practices that support and invest in one another as opposed to destroying or tearing down.

Autonomy is the practice of mobility. Acts of moving and traveling without being criminalized, incarcerated, or killed. The act of developing relationships with people, land, environments, and hubs. The practice of existing in place that are not our own.

Autonomy as a practice of self sufficiency without having to rely on nation/state for food, housing, medicine and survivability.

Autonomy as a practice of educating, teaching, and learning

knowledges and skills that will improve the conditions of our communities.

Autonomy as a practice of collective living where the people decide what is best for communities.

Autonomy as having the materials that we need to ensure the survivability of our communities.

Autonomy as a networks of families, peoples, organizations, communities working together.

Autonomy as a relationship with the earth, elements, and unknown mysteries.

—Albuquerque, New Mexico

* * *

from Chiapas Support Committee

Our discussion of autonomy highlights various facets of autonomy, which we list below, not in any particular order.

Values: Autonomy has to do with a group of people deciding that they want to live according to different values than the dominant culture. They need to have their own alternative cultural values, and a common agreement as to how to live in a place. Autonomy includes relationships to the animals and the environment. The core values are passed on to future generations.

Non-capitalistic economic models: Autonomy involves a way creating and distributing the necessities of life in a way that is not driven by profit, and must involve a more collective form of governance.

Creating your own systems: The Zapatistas created education, health, and justice systems, based on their specific needs and values.

Individual/collective: We have to change ourselves internally A key aspect to autonomy for the Zapatistas is that everybody puts the community before the individual. As oppressed people we feel defeated, like we don't have the voice or the power not to be at the mercy of money or power. We need to have agency to live and make our own decisions and choices collectively.

A practice, not a thing: Autonomy is not a set thing to aspire to, but an attitude, a process and a practice that involves both individuals and collectives. What can we do in our lives that can take us towards autonomy? For example, a part of the process would be to obstruct capitalist consumption, to find ways to stop prioritizing work, in other words, to reduce the amount of alienated labor we have to engage in. Abolishing the police in our communities is also an example of a move towards autonomy.

Four types of autonomy: organizational, institutional, movement and peoplehood. Autonomy for Zapatistas was a political evolution due to the failure of negotiations with the state. Autonomy is a political concept, but it could only happen when people are involved.

Examples of autonomy: Zapatistas, Rojava, Mujer Obrera (they have land, systems to generate income), Highlander Institute in Tennessee. Others are building autonomy through food justice based on the land. During COVID, groups organized with local farmers to distribute organic greens to those in need.

Reimbodiment, spirituality: Autonomy is the rebuilding that happens after the destruction of capitalist structures and the disembodiment that it creates. This re-embodiment has to include a spiritual journey.

Diversity: Autonomy will be diverse, depending on the circumstances, needs and desires of the communities involved, and de-centralized. Not all autonomies will look the same, autonomy will take different forms in different cultures. It is a long and hard process, so we have to be gentle in approaching it.

Visualizing autonomy: We need to create a space to visualize what our economy can look like outside of a capitalist system. How can Zapatista forms of autonomy be translated into an urban context? Our group is dispersed over a large urban area. We don't share land or space. As a collective one thing we can work towards is what does a material basis look like for us: do we want to buy land, do we want to open a co-op? We don't have land or space, but we can support and network with those who do, and build collectives. These are key to building autonomy.

—Oakland, California

* * *

from Autonomia Xochitequio

In our collective conversations and activities, we have been able to identify some fundamental points on the question of autonomy.

In principle, we have reached consensus that autonomy is, in its most general description, a practice that generates tools to open paths to ways of existing and relating to the world that are not imposed. As a practice, autonomy is put into *action* both **from *thought* and from doing**. Both questions present themselves as exercises, and, whether they are material or immaterial, each allows the other to appear. In this way, we have been able to verify that thinking and doing have been constantly separated in the West, but that it is necessary to think of them together, in a dialogue and interrelation, as the key to their disruptive and creative potential.

This being the case, we believe that **thought**, as a practice, is fundamental insofar

de Autonomia Xochitequio

En nuestras conversaciones y actividades colectivas, hemos podido reconocer algunos puntos fundamentales sobre la cuestión de la autonomía.

En principio, hemos llegado al consenso de que la autonomía es, en su descripción más general, una práctica que genera herramientas para abrir caminos a modos de existencia y relación con el mundo no impuestos. Como una práctica, la autonomía se pondría en *acto* tanto **desde el *pensamiento* como desde el hacer**. Ambas cuestiones se nos presentan como ejercicios y, aunque sean materiales o inmateriales, permiten uno al otro su aparición. De tal forma, hemos podido comprobar que el pensar y el hacer han estado constantemente separadas en Occidente, pero que es necesario pensarlas en conjunto, en un diálogo e interrelación, como la clave de su potencial disruptivo y creativo.

Siendo así, creemos que el **pensamiento**, como una práctica, es fundamental en tanto que se

as a critical vision and reflection of the world is needed to be able to understand, on the one hand, our place in the organization of society and, at the same time, how to project modes of resistance, problematization, and alternatives to it. In this sense, we understand that some sites of *intellectual knowledge*, whether produced by academics, militants, and/or collectives, help us understand that the hegemonic form of the world has capitalism as its center of gravity and that, through constant depredation and annihilation of the earth and its population, capitalism produces a generalized precariousness of life that benefits corporations and international banking. Understanding the mode of operation and deployment of the capitalist system, in its different modalities of functioning and productivization of life (e.g., sexual, racial, labor, state, economic, legislative), allows us to project, plan, imagine and observe, together, critical alternatives to its operation, from our specific territorial and social experience. From *action*, on the other hand, since a theoretical

necesita de una visión y reflexión crítica del mundo para poder entender, por un lado, cuál es nuestro lugar en la ordenación de la sociedad y, al mismo tiempo, cómo proyectar modos de resistencia, problematización y alternativa a la misma. En este sentido, entendemos que algunos lugares del *saber intelectual*, ya sean producidos por algunxs académicos, militantes y/o colectivos, nos ayudan a comprender que la forma hegemónica del mundo tiene al capitalismo como su centro de gravedad y que, a través de su constante depredación y aniquilación de la tierra y su población, produce una precarización generalizada de la vida para el beneficio de las empresas y la banca internacional. El comprender el modo de funcionamiento y despliegue del sistema capitalista, en sus distintos modos de funcionamiento y productivización de la vida (sexual, racial, laboral, estatal, económico, legislativo, etc.), nos permite proyectar, planear, imaginar y observar en conjunto alternativas críticas a su funcionamiento, desde nuestra experiencia territorial y social específica. Desde el *hacer*, por otro lado, ya que no bastaría

verification of the widespread crisis to which capital inevitably leads is not enough, it is necessary to *practice and materialize* alternatives to its order that, from different ways and degrees, erodes the given field of relationships and gives collectives the ability to make decisions about their own experiences and ways of relating. On various occasions, these practices in their daily weaving and unfolding teach us about *non-imposing* ways to meet and dialogue that allow unforeseen relationships to develop and other existing ways of knowing, ones that do not respond to the Western order, to be affirmed.

In accordance with all of the above, we also believe that autonomy is a practice that is carried out both collectively and individually. In this way, it is essential that the community, through the self-understanding of its forms, enables space where the traditional modes of producing social relations can be suspended, or, in other cases, uses of the same traditional modes to develop possible alternative ways of meeting and socializing. It is from this collective perspective

solo con una constatación teórica de la crisis extendida a la que nos lleva inevitablemente el Capital, sino que sería necesario *practicar y materializar* alternativas a su orden que, desde distintos modos y grados, erosiones el campo de relaciones dado y entregue a las colectividades la capacidad de decisión sobre sus propias experiencias y modos de relación. En variadas ocasiones, estas prácticas nos enseñan en su despliegue y tejido cotidiano, sobre modos de encuentro y diálogo *no impositivos* que permiten el desarrollo de relaciones no previstas y la afirmación de otros modos de saber existente que no responde al orden Occidental.

En concordancia con todo lo anterior, creemos también que la autonomía es una práctica que se lleva a cabo tanto colectiva como individualmente. De tal manera, es fundamental constatar que la colectividad posibilita, en la autocomprensión de sus formas, un espacio donde se pueden poner en suspenso los modos tradicionales de relación productiva de lo social, o, en otros caso, utilizar estos mismos modos tradicionales para la elaboración de alternativas de encuentro y socialización

that we open ourselves to an alternative relationship with the land, production, social hierarchies, history, culture, and other instances that germinate in our collaboration and dialogue. All this allows us, at the same time, to problematize individual practices that reproduce the same order of representations and social beliefs, making it possible to re-evaluate and re-comprehend the standards we live by as well as our beliefs, to open ourselves to the possibility of practicing new ideas that don't need to be imposed on others or ourselves.

Our own practice of autonomy arises from the specific geographic context of the border between the United States and Mexico, in the urban sprawl that encompasses San Diego and Tijuana, on occupied Kumeyaay territory that was never ceded. Within this geographic expanse we travel between centers of military and technological power that make San Diego their home and the underworlds that sustain these centers. It is in the interstices are areas of dispossession where excess materials, excess waste, and excess people accumulate. Our

posible. Es, desde esta perspectiva colectiva, que nos abrimos a una relación alternativa con la tierra, la producción, las jerarquías sociales, la historia, la cultura y muchas otras instancias, las cuales germinan en nuestra colaboración y diálogo. Todo esto nos permite, a mismo tiempo, problematizar nuestras prácticas individuales que reproducen el mismo orden de representaciones y creencias sociales, haciendo posible reevaluar y re-comprender los estándares de nuestra vida y nuestras creencias, para abrirnos a la posibilidad de practicar nuevas ideas, sin necesidad de ser impuestas ni a otros, ni a nosotrxs mismxs.

Nuestra propia práctica de la autonomía surge desde el contexto geográfico específico de la frontera entre EEUU y México, en el despliegue urbano que abarca San Diego Y Tijuana, ocupando territorio Kumeyaay nunca cedido. Entre dicha extensión geográfica transitamos entre centros de poder militar y tecnológicos que hacen de San Diego su hogar, al igual que los inframundos que sustentan estos centros. En las interstices ocupan zonas de despojo, donde se acumulan materiales que sobran,

journeys reveal the environmental and affective catastrophe that these sacrificial zones generate, and from these places we seek to generate an infrastructure that sustains life. As a practice of autonomy, the *rascuache* appropriates and revalues what has been dispossessed and puts those very discards back into circulation. This time, not in the service of an incessant accumulation of capital, but of a collective material and spiritual sustenance.

Rascuacheando, we get down to work, in a way that precludes the demands for efficiency that capital imposes.

The trajectory inscribed in the form of the broken and discarded materials that we recover needs to be unraveled. We dismember wooden fences, transmute food that was allowed to rot, crush cans that were on their way to the dump. The rebuilding process arises as a collective and creative effort that transforms us as well as the material.

In short, the practice of autonomy, from its different places of intervention, invites us to a different way of engaging with the world, keeping in mind

desechos que sobran y gente que sobra. Nuestro caminar reconoce la catástrofe ambiental y afectiva que generan estas zonas sacrificiales, y desde estos sitios busca generar una infraestructura que sustente la vida. Como práctica de la autonomía, lo "rascuache", retoma y revaloriza lo despojado y vuelve a poner en circulación esos mismos desechos. Esta vez, no al servicio de una acumulación de Capital incessante, sino de un sustento colectivo material y espiritual.

"Rascuacheando" ponemos manos a la obra, de una forma que requiere obviar las demandas de eficiencia que impone el Capital.

Al tomar materiales rotos y descartados necesitamos deshacer su trayectoria inscrita en su forma. Descuartizamos vallas de madera, transmutamos comida que se dejó pudrir, y aplastamos latas que iban en camino a ser enterradas. El proceso de reconstruir surge como un esfuerzo colectivo y creativo que nos transforma a nosotrxs al igual que al material.

En definitiva, la práctica de la autonomía, desde sus distintos lugares de intervención, nos invita a llevar a cabo otra relación con el mundo, teniendo a la vista las

the critical experiences that already exist and are unfolding within it. Learning from its forms and putting into practice transformations in our daily lives, both collectively and individually.

—San Diego, CA
(Kumeyaay territory)

experiencias críticas que en él ya existen y se despliegan. Aprendiendo de sus formas y poniendo en práctica transformaciones en nuestro cotidiano, tanto colectiva como individualmente.

—San Diego, CA
(territorio Kumeyaay)

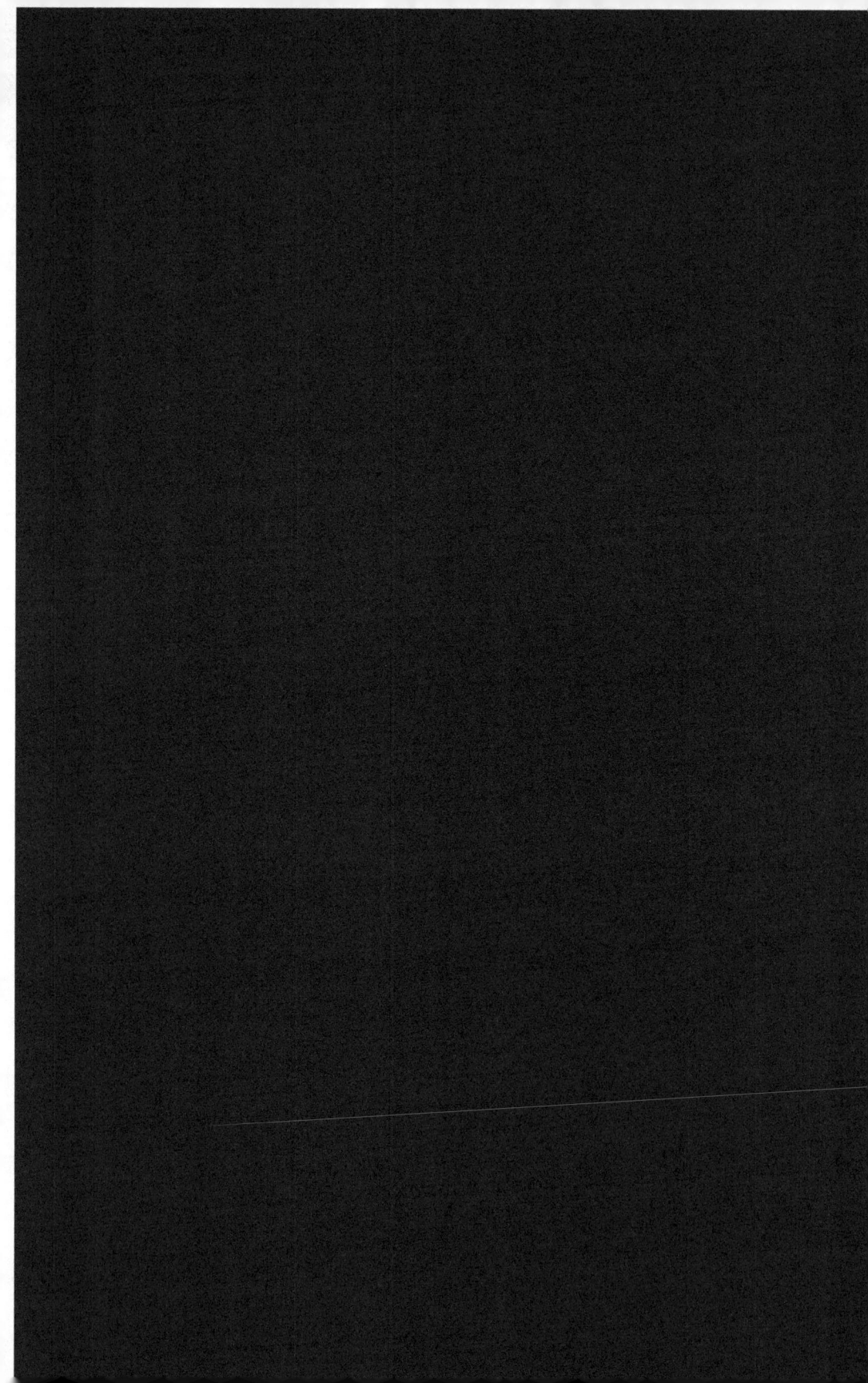

Ashanti Alston
Speech at AK Press (2006)

First thing: *Power to the people!*

[AUDIENCE RESPONSE: Power to the people!]

What we usually say when someone says, "Power to the people," the response is, "*All* power to the people," alright? But "all power" means that all power goes to the people, right? Didn't say "to the party," didn't say "to the state," it didn't say "to the slick talkers" and all the other ones. *To the people, to the people, to the people*, alright? So for me, it's like, it's very anarchistic, you know? To the people, right? *Power to the people!*

[AUDIENCE RESPONSE: All power to the people!]

Right on, that's pretty good...

What we're going to try to do tonight is to talk about our experience in Chiapas—this was last year, though, so this was all before the *Sixth Declaration*. And a lot of the things that are going on with the *Sixth Declaration* I am still trying to understand. I have not formulated any analysis, any positions, I am just open to what's going on there, and especially hearing people's interpretations when they go and come back, or the things that I can find on the internet, I'm trying to understand. But this is still, for me, one of the most exciting struggles that has been going on probably since the Spanish Civil War, early days of the Chinese Revolution, early days of maybe even the Cuban and maybe some of the African liberation movements and other Third World liberation movements—this is exciting stuff happening here!

And it's why it's exciting to me that brings in my past, in terms of the Black Panther Party. I think it's important because we're still engaged in this project here of making revolution in the United States. And I smile when I say revolution because I love the word revolution. I just learned to change "Big R" revolution to "small r" revolution, and I'll probably get into some of that today because for me, that's a big step coming from a time period where "revolution" meant that there was a particular way that you had to think/organize/fight; with a particular plan that led to a particular goal that would look like a particular thing—whether we called it socialism, communism, whatever,

> We're still engaged in this project here of making revolution in the United States.

you know? And to go through so many changes in my own lifetime, to being open to learning, to come to the conclusion like the Zapatistas, that there are no "plans." There are no "final plans", there is no "Big R" revolution, there has never really been one that has succeeded.

But small revolution means that the small people get to make this revolution happen; they bring in their creativity, they bring in their diversity, coming from different places in life, different experiences, different knowledge bases, means that no one can come and say, "Well I got it all. You just got to follow me, you just got to follow our organization. You just got to see our vision." So for me, this Zapatista revolution becomes what we could've done in the 1960s, at our height, that is what I see the Zapatistas doing now. Their vision, their style of working with people, how they draw from their own cultures, how they're open to pulling knowledge and information from other areas of the world and all of this stuff they do. And so I look at the things we did in the Panther Party and say, "Man, I wish I could've done this, I wish we could've done that, maybe we wouldn't have lost," you know?

Coming from a small Black town in New Jersey—Plainfield, NJ— "Black Power" was what pushed a lot of us young people to more radical positions. Before that, the Civil Rights Movement held sway and it was all about integrating into the Empire. A lot of us were learning from Malcolm X and looking at some of the other struggles going on in the world, and it was like, why do we want to integrate ourselves into a capitalist society that is thoroughly racist and killing us—what is this thing abut wanting a piece of the pie? So from them kind of inspirations we looked for different information. And at the time, it was 1968 May in France, it was the struggle of the Vietnamese from the French to the United States. The Third World Liberation Movements were giving us ideas, new ways to go. And for a lot of us to be exposed to socialism, communism, and Marxism, that was really, really great stuff at the time. And for someone like me who was just an average high school student—not really great, not really interested in reading, the Black Panther Party found me at a time when it made learning one of the most exciting things in the world. But learning about how to create freedom. How to build our own power bases. How to take our lives back, in that time period.

We did our best. And when I say we did our best, we organized; not only our community, but so many different communities were inspired to organize, so it wasn't just us. It was the Latino communities, the Asian communities, workers was doing their thing, women were doing their thing, the anti-war movement was strong. It just seemed like this was a time of possibilities—anything was possible! We just had to figure out how to come together and do it. The Black Panther Party stood out from a lot of the revolutionary Black Nationalist groups—what we called ourselves— because we was about working with anybody who was down with this idea of revolution, who was down with this idea of liberation for the different communities within the Empire. We worked with everyone, from poor whites in the Appalachian mountains to our Puerto Rican neighbors— like for me, coming from New York or New Jersey, we all lived side by side. And it made sense that the Puerto Ricans who were fighting for independence of their island, though they may have lived in New York or New Jersey, independence was their objective. And for those of us fighting for Black Power in our communities in the United States, it made sense that we would bond together. And that was happening in different ways and different expressions all over the country. And it was happening in different ways and different expressions all over the world.

But one of the things that I do think weakened us was that it got to a point where we saw that there had to be one way, one path, to revolution. Marxism, Leninism, even maybe Trotskyism and others did play a big part in that, but it was the idea of a scientific revolution; that you had to think scientifically, that if we held to the correct analysis and organized amongst specific groups that was designated as the only revolutionary class or group that could do this, that would lead us to this final objective of freedom, communism, socialism—wonderful terms, but all that was taking away from these different individual struggles' own integrity. And what I mean by that is that not all of us was really buying into that it just had to be one way. Native American and Indigenous people here was like, they didn't want to hear that stuff. Like the Indigenous people of Mexico, they had their own ways of understanding the world. And they wanted that to be respected, but I think that one of the mistakes we made was that we was trying to push everybody: one-way revolution, "Big R" revolution. That, and what the counterintelligence program was doing—and the counterintelligence program was merely playing on our own weaknesses, on our own contradictions, it did what it was supposed to do. It made sure that we fell. That we destroyed ourselves. And it's always better to get the oppressed to do that—when it looks like they're destroying themselves by their own hands, rather than to have the government, CIA and others do it. So that's why it always looks better for Black hands to shoot Malcolm X rather than some white FBI, some white police, you know? Because it affects us more in our spirits when it seems to happen from our own hands. And they know what they're doing because they have been crushing revolutions all around the world.

What was important for me was being a part of an experiment in changing the world. It inspired me, it inspired so many other people. I was a Panther, a field worker, on the ground, organizing. A Panther on the ground who was brought up believing that "n*ggas ain't shit," "n*ggas will never organize," "they will never unite," "never, never, never, never, never do anything positive." Now, here comes the Panthers who got programs with Black people feeding Black children, Black people providing clothing for Black people—well, anybody actually, in that neighborhood area was getting fed, whether you was Black, white, you know, of color. Didn't matter. Free clinics, right? Liberation schools, and the whole idea was that

What was important for me was being a part of an experiment in changing the world.

we could do for ourselves. To live it, and to take those kinds of risks, where you are actually serving each other, destroys all the myths that you were brought up on, you know? So no longer was it "n*ggas ain't shit," it was "we are Black people," we are "people of African descent," "Africa is our roots," "Black is beautiful. That was heady stuff. That was stuff that was not only cleansing us, but it was giving us a nurturing that made us feel like nothing was impossible. But again: FBI, the Counter Intelligence Program, the local police departments, people's fears in your community, the media's role in shaping people's thoughts all played a part into frustrating our efforts to keep this revolution building, building, and building. So by 1970, '74 maybe the early '70s, for all intents and purposes, there were no more revolutionary movements. They were on decline which meant that a lot of us might have been on the run. Or just trying to hold together the movement from an underground position. And I was one of those who was trying to hold it together from an underground position, because at some point I was recruited into the ranks of the Black Liberation Army.

Never was the Black Liberation Army a figment of our thoughts, it was very real. It was a part of the Black Liberation Movement. And when we went underground and we took up arms, we were part of a movement, an army that was the same as the Chinese Liberation Army, that was the same as the Tupamaros, that was the same as the MLPA in Angola. We saw ourselves as developing that armed force within the United States that could protect those of us who were activists in the communities, and also to help promote through financial means whatever our needs were. So that means that yeah, the banks, we rolled into them banks. Yeah, and we went in there and we made withdrawals, right? We did not call what we did robberies, so we didn't say bank robberies, we had a fancy term and I think it was a Marxist term, too. We called it expropriations. And our feeling was that banks were just those institutions that sucked the blood of people, and that's how they got their money. So we was just getting monies that came from us some other way anyhow. The whole thing was to put it back into the movement. And that's what we did. Dope dealers got the same thing. We was that force, like especially in Harlem and in parts of Newark, where we hit the dope dealers. Dope dealers felt our sting because we took their drugs, we destroyed their drugs, we took their money and their money also went into programs in the communities.

We understood that even as guerillas, urban guerillas in America, in the United States, we had to help fund ourselves. We were not waiting for the Open Society Institute and that guy George Soros to fund our revolution. There was not a movement that had any kind of success that did not find ways of funding themselves. But you had to have a certain daringness to do that. And I think one of the successes of the Black Panther Party is that it reached into our society and got those groups of people who had that kind of daringness. That was that lumpen-proletariat as we called it, right? That was people who had already been in a kind of combative relationship with society. That gave the Black Panther Party so many advantages, because you had people who didn't work, or didn't do any work that had any meaningful part in production, but who were willing to learn because they was on the bottom. They were willing to like, break out of old role models that said that we couldn't do anything, and in the organizational arms of the Black Panther Party, we found ourselves doing stuff that we never thought we could do.

People started coming to us, wanting to join, wanting to support. It created such a concern for the FBI that they declared us Public Enemy Number One. But that's what

> We understood that even as guerillas, urban guerillas in America, in the United States, we had to help fund ourselves.

it's supposed to do when people are effectively organizing, anywhere, but it's gotta be a result of the work that we do. When people start pulling each other out of the system, out of the system's ways of thinking, of course the system is going to get concerned. And it's going to throw all of its forces into disrupting that. And it did that with us. But I think that [they succeeded], partly, not only because of the rigidness of some of the ideas that we took, but because we were young and inexperienced and they were very experienced in what they did. So, we were amongst other groups that were destroyed.

After that, a lot of us went to prison. Some had to leave the country and go into exile. Many were killed. But even more, their lives were destroyed, even to this day, some who are still alive are just like, walking dead because they done lost their minds, you know? Or they went to drugs or alcohol to just dull the pain, you know? All of that stuff. But those of us who went to prison, we kept on reading and kept on reading and kept on analyzing, kept on looking at our struggles from different lenses.

Like for me, for example, when I went to prison I started reading radical psychology. I started reading feminism. I started reading Erich Fromm and Marcuse, and people from the Frankfurt School, people I ain't never even heard of before, but they were giving me different ways to look at what has just happened with our struggle. All of that was

> We found ourselves doing stuff that we never thought we could do.

leading me to try to find different forms of struggle that may give us a better chance at developing. That maybe we wouldn't create the same problems that we had in the past: How do we get away from hierarchy? How do we create organizations that don't silence women? That ain't shutting out those who are queer? Or the ageist stuff that goes on; because we was all young, we didn't even want to deal with nobody over 30, 35, you know? Even today it seems like it's just the reverse, it's that the older ones don't want to deal with young people.

But it was like, how can we create organizations that somehow reflect the kind of society that we want? And continually build, continually find ways to sustain ourselves so that we can eventually take back chunks and chunks and chunks of our lives. Coming out of prison, you come out with all these ideas. But one of the things about coming out of prison is that you're coming back into, like, a vacuum. I was in from '74 to '86. In that time period it seemed like people didn't even know about the Panthers, didn't know about the Weather Underground, didn't know about the anti-war movement, the women's movement, the Native Americans, the Chicano struggles, the Puerto Rican independence movement, didn't know! And you get a sense that the system was very effective at seemingly erasing all of this knowledge.

So we walk around, we're out here now and there's not much organizing going on—what can we do for the political prisoners, those who are still in? Not much going on. My spirits would be up, sometimes down, up, sometimes down. Through the '80s, the rest of the '80s I did things for political prisoners with just the few handful that was also doing it, right? Here comes the '90s; the Panthers from the west coast, and Panthers from the east coast finally started talking again. And we came across an idea that we wanted to put out the newspaper, so the early '90s was this effort of Panthers from the east and west coast getting together and we got a newspaper. Young people see the newspaper and they want to know about the Panthers. Now we got a Black Panther collective, and other people was forming other organizations. Sometimes it did well, sometimes it didn't. Spirits go up, spirits go down. For several years, my spirits was like "Oh, man I wonder if we're going to do this?" you know?

Then 1994,
January 1st
happens.

It's like a blast
from outta
nowhere.

Some people,
some Brown
people in the
southeastern
mountains of
Mexico just had
an uprising.

Then 1994, January 1st happens. It's like a blast from outta nowhere. Some people, some Brown people in the southeastern mountains of Mexico just had an uprising. They just took over all this land, they just kicked out the Mexican police, kicked out the military. And did it in such a flamboyant way. It was like "Woah!" If these people can do this, and not have all the resources and technologies that we have here and always claiming that we ain't got no money, we can't do this, can't do that, and they have found a way to take back their lives, then revolution is back on the agenda, you know? And then the more you find out about them, you get into more of their thinking, yeah, you find out more about [Subcomandante Insurgente] Marcos but you get more into their thinking, and how they're viewing things. Why is this guerrilla organization not fighting to capture state power? Why is this armed guerrilla organization doing things that don't seem to focus so much on their guns? But it's clear that they're not putting their guns down. Different from the Tupamaros, different from a lot of the other guerrilla organizations, whether it was the Red Brigades or whatever. For me, it was exciting, because I know that our attempts to use guerrilla warfare to aid the community movements wasn't really effective, right? I know also that groups' efforts to come up with the "grand solutions" wasn't really the way to go. So now here are these Zapatistas saying it ain't really about the "grand

solutions." It's not really about the gun, but we knew that in the days of the '60s too, 'cause we always said "politics in command," but I think we kinda lost sight of that.

So here was a group saying we have a vision that comes from our sense of dignity. And they put this thing about dignity in the core of their thinking, and it made me think back to like the '60s, like the early '60s up to the late '60s, a lot of the Black groups would talk about dignity. And maybe we got away something when that started changing when then we started talking about the more scientific concepts, right? But to believe that all you need to be free should be grounded in your sense of dignity, what makes for a dignified life. It was simple, but it was like fantastic, you know? So we read more, and all the stuff we could get. I went the first time with a couple of anarchists from the ABC (Anarchist Black Cross), Bronx. And they were taking medical supplies to the Zapatistas. And they knew I was excited about the Zapatistas so it was like, "Ashanti, do you want to go to Mexico with us?" I'm like ,"Yo, I ain't got no money, I'd like to go but, you know..." And they say, "OK don't worry about it, we'll raise some money." Now at first, I'm like "yeah, OK." But when they finally got the tickets, I was actually scared. 'Cause I didn't really think this was gonna happen. Then, it's going to be the first time I'm going to be outside of the country. But I'm like "Ain't no way I'm turning this down." So we go. And we go to San Cristobal, and then from there, most of our time was in La Realidad—even the name was like blowing my mind—The Reality! This is their territory, they have named it and claimed it! And who could not come in? The police, the army, the corporations. My mind would go immediately back to the United States, right? And I'm like "why can't we do that!?" Alright, so we're not gonna do it in no mountainous rural area, because we don't have that. But it's about autonomy; autonomy is applicable anywhere. It would be our responsibility to figure out how to apply it in the United States—in a Brooklyn, in a Harlem, in an Oakland, you know? That would be our responsibility.

So it's like, "I'm here, I'm gonna learn as much as I can." We had a chance—I'm glad there was interpreters, because my knowledge of Spanish was very, very small. But it was such a great learning experience for me

because it solidified so many things I had
been questioning myself about—can a struggle
happen in a way that makes itself open to
different ideas, that demands the respect of not
only diversity, but everyone coming into this
diversity? Here are Indigenous people that
spoke different languages, but created a space
where they could work that stuff out and come
to some common visions. It made me think
about, I think it was 1970, the Revolutionary
People's Constitutional Convention that the
Panthers kind of initiated, which brought
together so many of the different groups
within the United States, with the objective of
writing a new constitution. The Zapatistas was
doing this, and diversity became not a negative
thing but it became this really positive thing.

They said, "Walking we ask questions."

That blew my mind.

Automatically I'm thinking, in the United
States we got so many differences that we
make negative, there's so many groups that
just want to vie for leadership. Here's the
Zapatistas, the hottest thing going on in the
society, that created space and say, "This space
is for all those who are oppressed, for us to
come and to try to figure out what's the next
step." That blew my mind, right? They said,
"Walking, we ask questions," right? That blew
my mind. It was almost like, you know—I
don't even know if I should say it like this—
you know you go into a Chinese restaurant
and you get the fortune cookies and you open
them up and it has this little saying, sometimes
it's very profound. And they were saying this
stuff that is like very profound but so fuckin'

Ashanti Alston Speech at AK Press (2006)

simple. We do not have a way of figuring out this revolution beforehand; walking we'll ask questions. We'll turn to each other, for the first time with some humility and say, "What do you know, what do you know? Let's put it on the table. Let's raise some questions."

With the Zapatistas the questions become more important than whatever your so-called factual stuff is, right? Create a world where many worlds can fit—I'm like, "Oh shit!" The United States—how can we do it? You got Indigenous nations right in the United States. You got Black folks who identify with a concept called Black Nation. You got Chicanos who identify with Aztlan. You got workers who want dignified lives that really come down to meaning that they should be owning and controlling the means of their production, whatever they work in. And trying to figure out how to fit that into a whole new social scheme that can serve everybody, you know? You got queer folks who are trying to create a world that's for them, with them and involved with all other kinds of worlds, and I'm like "Damn!" And it meant for me, getting involved with this, that I had to interact with a lot of new people, and every interaction was a new lesson. But that seemed to be the whole idea of the Zapatistas: everything should be a new lesson. Everything should be a way to see another piece of the puzzle, to clear out some of the confusion or the smoke around here and there, and try to create some kind of mechanisms where you can get another piece

> Create a world where many worlds fit   I'm like, "Oh shit!" The United States   how can we do it?

of your life back, where you can take control of another piece of your life.

For me it became one of the most important struggles that I—I'm just glad that, being alive now, I thought the '60s was that period where—I used to always say, "It was the greatest period that ever existed in this country," but I'm convinced that now is that period. Because it's not only the Zapatistas, you got all other kind of struggles that's going on in the world, and even right here, of people trying different ways of doing different activities to take back their lives, to think differently, coming up with new concepts. Like I'm one of them that likes a lot of post-modernist stuff, but me trying to read that stuff man, was like ugh... I would go get the dictionary, the standard Webster's stuff, and none of the words would even exist in the dictionary, you know? So now the next thing I gotta do is google, 'cause I love the fact—I love googling, it's the only thing that probably keeps me on the computer. But now I'm understanding so many more concepts, like hegemony, territorialization, and de-territorialization, and at first I'm like, "Why the fuck they gotta use these big words?" when I'm sure there's some simple words to do it. But in trying and me pushing it, because that's the exciting thing for me: if I don't know, I gotta do some digging. But a lot of the reason for why I'm trying to get this is because I also was trying to understand more of the Zapatista struggle, and a lot of these other struggles going on around the world, and what the radical academics were saying about them, and when what we were saying about them in the grassroots.

And some of the radical academics, the radical postmodernists, was trying to make that bridge between them and us, to make that stuff more understandable, and that tended to be the stuff that I would drift towards. But it made me realize that the concepts that were used in the '60s and the '70s—that stuff didn't work no more, right? The ways that we thought about raising consciousness, that stuff didn't work no more. Handing a flyer to somebody, you know, saying, "Come to this meeting, come to this rally, come to this talk," you know? The struggle takes more than that, 'cause you're talking to real human beings, you know? And that was that thing again that brought me back to what the Zapatistas were saying about dignity; us realizing that we're all human beings, and what does that mean?

That means that human beings can think, they feel, they have dreams, they have desires, they have fears, you know? Let's figure out ways to deal with this whole person now and not just this "political actor" who is just supposed to come to the organization and unite with you and all this other stuff. So in these Zapatista communities, when we would go, you get to see in practice how people are living their autonomy. You get to see how they're living this new kind of "small r" revolution.

This last time we went, we would go to say, Oventik, which is one of the autonomous municipalities, it's kind of like their administrative area and it's regular folks from these communities who may sit on the Junta. And when we first heard the word *junta*, you automatically assume that this is them juntas, like the military dictators! But then somebody says, no, just deal with the definition of the word. The junta that we're used to is what the United States has always supported and we thought that was the definition. But it's just an assembly of people, and you go in here and you sit before the Zapatista community, the Junta in particular, and you're looking at the folks and they're regular people, except that they all have notebooks and pens and they're taking copious notes of everything that we're saying, the whole conversation. And the reason they're doing that is because during this two-week term that they're gonna be on the Junta, they wanna make sure they understand what is being communicated, they're making sure that they jot down any decisions that's made, so that when their term is over and the next crew comes on, they can look at the notes and see what went on before.

And this was this thing they was calling "rotating leadership," and I'm like "man, that's all the stuff I was reading in anarchism." They don't even call themselves anarchists, but they're doing this stuff in practice. They do not get caught up in the terms. I'm like, "Right on!" Because their lives is in this position where they must figure out ways of making decisions, of sustaining themselves, of being a part of participating. And the Zapatistas want everyone to participate, so people come on here who have never been in a leadership position before, and now here they are trying their hands. It's got to be not only scary for them, in a way, but it's got to be a wonderful experience for them, too. To see that it wasn't always—"the leadership thing"—that terrifying anyhow. Participation is really a doable, but the more people who participate and get this experience, the less likely it is that this particular struggle can be reversed. 'Cause to get a feeling of what autonomy is like, what it means to have that power in your hands for communities, for yourselves, that's some really, it's some really great stuff.

I come right back to my thinking of the United States. It made me think of groups that are already exercising that kind of autonomy in different communities I've been in, but it also showed me that we could bring lessons like that back home. How could I bring that to a Harlem that's being gentrified? My first thing would be just to look for those folks in the community who are already practicing some form of autonomy— don't even know the word, don't even care about the word, but already in their communities, whether it's how to protect their neighborhood, how to take care of each others children, you know? How they're feeding each other, how they're making ends meet when the money runs out from the public assistance. They just need to see that that's it, that is a beginning. And to make this thing work to liberate all of your lives, just think about how it can begin to expand, you know? And that's the things that I would learn when we went to the different Zapatista communities, is that you start simple, you start small, you start with what you know and what you already do. You don't really even have to, from people coming from the outside, create something different. There's a lot of stuff going on right now, right in people's lives, and you're just trying to get them to see that you've already got control, figure out how to get more.

And Critical Resistance in New York, we're pushing this thing called a "Harm-Free Zone," which is basically we want people to stop dialing 911, right? If there's an issue in the community—a fight, you know? Domestic violence; women feeling that their bodies are in danger and there may be high incidents of rape, where can we set up things where they feel safety, they can go in case they feel like that. We want people to see that even something simple like that, kids are fighting in the street? Intervene. And if the intervention is scary, then figure out how to do it in community with other people, so that even though it's scary, you'll take the steps anyhow, and you'll see that it gets easier just like learning to swim or any other thing. You might be afraid at first, but you know we can still do it. The fear doesn't have to stop us. And it made me also ask in the Zapatista communities of folks who I sensed were veterans, "How was it in the beginning? How was it when you first started?" And it's usually the same stories: people are afraid, people are scared. And the only way they was able to help people to overcome was to be a continuing presence there and working with people around particular issues that affected their lives.

And their issues are going to be different, right? But the whole key was you start with their issues. And we all know the story now, like when the intellectuals who helped to form the Zapatistas came from the universities with all their highfalutin ideas, you know? And they go to Indigenous folks and the Indigenous folks ain't havin' it! You know, they don't want to be preached to, they don't wanna hear about no Marxist-Leninist-Maoist Revolution, organizing the workers. They had their own ideas. So it was like sitting all of them folks down, from Marcos and others, and saying "Yo, chill with that stuff," you know? It's not that we're opposed, but we've been living here for generations, we've been sizing up our world and our worlds for generations, we know how to do this, we know how to size up that. If you got something to offer, let's sit down as equals but don't talk to us like we're idiots, you know? Which is what we tended to do, even in the '60s and '70s, and groups still do, believe it or not, to this day. It's unbelievable that a group will come today with a whole revolutionary thing worked out in their head and they just stand around you and be like, "Join my organization," you know? "This is the plan, this is the way to do it, organize the workers," you know? The Zapatistas was like a coming together of folks of different knowledges that figured out a way to pull from the strengths of both.

So now they can understand this post-modern world that has aspects of pre-postmodern, modern, postmodern, all that stuff, right? I'm excited by that stuff, but I can't talk it that good, right? It's difficult. But, it helped me to understand that we should not be trying to destroy other folks who we feel like, because they think different, and they're not "scientific," that they need to be changed and our goal is to change them, you know? This Zapatista revolution was something that was pulling together so many strings for me, around so many questions that I had as to why we could not carry ours in the '60s and the '70s. They was giving me ways to go, and then to be able to find others, you know? And the first time I went was with the two white women from the ABC Bronx. The second time I found out about Estación Libre, and Estación Libre was a group that—two individuals went down there and their experience down there, they met with some racism in terms of, a lot of the folks going was white folks, white activists. And some of the same things they experienced here they was experiencing down there. And so they wanted to get away from that space, and at the same time create a space where folks of color could like, go and interact on their own, without having to deal with the racism of the group that's taking you, you know?

So they got together—two individuals, just like the Black Panther Party, Huey P. Newton and Bobby Seale—two individuals get together and create something. And the reason I'm pointing out the two individuals is 'cause that's how things start. There's always the question of "how can we do this today?" or "How do we do that?" Two individuals. Get together. Talk. Figure out what you can do. But you've got to come together. There's nobody that's going to come and lay the answers down in your lap, figure that shit out, you know? That's what they did. Because to this day, one of the things that stands out about the Zapatistas' struggle is its Mayan-base, and its openness to other ideas, you know? But it's definitely a Mayan-based struggle. And it was great for me that

> The Indigenous folks ain't havin' it! You know, they don't want to be preached to, they don't wanna hear about no Marxist Leninist Maoist Revolution, organizing the workers. They had their own ideas.

these Mayans are Brown people, you know? Because like, for me, people of color in the United States, we are still battered every day. We still gotta deal every day with a bombardment of negative messages about who we are, and even the best of us sometimes have doubts about what we can do, as individuals, and as peoples, you know? And there's things you gotta do every day to kinda keep your spirits up, keep your sense of who you are together....

* * *

But I love the fact that the Zapatistas' concern is power being with people, that they decide how to do this, you know? And it's a really great thing. So we can figure it out as we go, but I think for me it's obvious that those ways we've tried to do it in the past have never worked. Never worked. There ain't been a successful revolution, I feel, to this day— Russian, Cuban, Chinese; I've got big respect for the Cuban people and even big respect for Fidel, right? But it's like, Mao and them all did the same thing. They became the new oppressors, you know? All that stuff changed. The rhetoric stayed the same...

* * *

One of the things I think the Zapatistas show is that nonviolent struggle is still doable. They just don't make it the "be all, end all." But it's like here, and everything draws me back here because I watch them, right? They use nonviolent struggle effectively, in combination with being an armed group, right? And it makes me think here, like, here we have not even used the tip of that iceberg of nonviolent struggle. All the things we can do, if you read Gene Sharp, and all these other things, we ain't even got creative with that, we just do basically the same two or three things, you know? But I mean even Gene Sharp, I mean his stuff was about how to like take over your lives, whether it's city blocks, neighborhoods, whatever. And that's what like the Zapatistas showed me, is that even if it was a group like the Black Panthers and the Black Liberation Army, you know, we could have played more of an effective role in promoting so many different forms of struggle. We got to the point where if you wasn't ready to pick up the gun, you wasn't even a real revolutionary, right? But you see them women—where was the women where they pushed out the soldiers? You see the Zapatista women, right? They, like the soldiers is in the community and they want their community back, and they are just physically pushing these soldiers out, you know? I'm like that takes so much courage! But it's creative too, you know? And I'm like damn, can we do something like that here? I always want to confront them, right? And really a lot of my wanting to confront—that's just the police and them, right?—because we've got so much fear of just these front-line troops. So much fear, you know? And sometimes just eyeball-to-eyeball looking at them takes a lot of courage. But it's a step. And even daring to think that we could really push them out of our neighborhoods, and all kind of ways just keep 'em out, you know? And so for me, I'm always a proponent of people arming their struggles, their communities. Because I know, as far as I'm convinced, that's always going to be a necessity. But it's like, you begin to realize it takes many forms of struggle.

That's why I like the whole thing with a lot of the anarchist-influenced struggles here, you know? From the convergences to the spokescouncils, all these other things, like diversity of tactics and all this other stuff, it's like we figure out ways of carrying these struggles the ways that we really think they need to be carried out, you know? And don't nobody come tell me that I cannot defend my community by any means necessary. I'm not gonna tell you that you can't block that bridge, but maybe we can figure out a way that you can block the bridge at the same time I wanna take over my community, we might can make that shit work, you know? How can we work our stuff, understanding that this system still is not gonna allow us to do shit that's going to threaten its power. But we wanna live, you know? As dangerous as it is to take that step and say "I'm going to confront these people," with all their new technology, their terrifying weapons, like Huey also says, you know, the spirit of the people is greater than "man's" technology, you know? I do believe that the people can defeat the most ferocious monster in the world. We can do this. We just need to really see how much is available to us in terms of the fight back.

*   *   *

I can tell you one of the things, like the Black Panthers, I think that the fact that we knew we was gonna have confrontations, even coming in. I came into the Black Panther Party at a time where it was just before the split in the Black Panther Party, so 1970, '71. There was Panthers that had already been driven underground, exiled, There was shootouts, people died on both sides. Yet here I am coming in 16, 17 years old. But it's like, it was easier because Plainfield, New Jersey was one of them where the police was always a presence, always fucking with you. You're always in combat, you know? With so many people who came into the Panther Party, in a certain way, were combat ready. One of my comrades in the BLA, in the cell that I was in, was a Vietnam veteran. Already combat ready, but then now you have—like this particular one I'm talking about—just to back up a little, I was a burglar, right? And even coming into the Panther Party I used the burglary skills, me and my closest comrade, we broke into the white communities outside of Plainfield—you know, Robin Hood stuff. You break in, you get stuff, you take it to the fence, you get money, you go get the food, and now in your lunch program for the kids. In one of them, you know, we got popped and stuff and all like that, but that's some of the things we did.

Going underground was the first time I was going to be introduced to weapons, right? And it's having that comrade that was a Vietnam veteran by my side, that gave me the courage even when I was scared to do some of the things that we had to do, you know? But it was the same, like when I was just a Panther Party field worker, you know, you got somebody with you who's a little bit more experienced, and they help to walk you through it, you know, and it becomes easier, and that just seems to work, you know? We've been raised to be terrified of the powers that be, so how do we break some of that down. We've gotta figure out ways, and all kind of ways, to confront. And sometimes it's just simple, like, Fanon would talk about, I think this is in his section of *Wretched of the Earth*, "On Violence", and there was this whole thing about how to kill the colonizer frees the colonized. For me, I mean, it can happen in many different ways. To even look your oppressor, your colonizer in the eyes frees you. Because, you know the whole thing even with Black people, it was hard—even to this day it's hard for a lot of us to look a white person in the eyes without the tendency to put your head down. Now you imagine the '60s, this was just before Black Power, Black is Beautiful. After that, you know, you had Black folks going up to white cops smacking them in the face! You know, it was a different time...

* * *

Sometimes that points to the colonization of activist thinking. And who's setting the standards for what's legitimate actions and what's not. And just a small thing, like, at the time of the Black Liberation Army, the Weather Underground and others, because so many on the left didn't like what we were doing, played a part in our isolation. You know? I mean the media, the government and all of them was already on the thing of isolating us, but because you got some problem with the way that we choose to fight back, you are also not gonna write about us or not gonna write about us accurately, just blot us out. Or just tell people that we're ultra leftists or, you know, anarchists, you know? And a lot of us wouldn't even accept the term anarchism back then, right? But it's like, you play a part, you know? You play a part. Just like in Seattle, when some folks was trying to catch those breaking the windows of—what's the coffee place? Starbucks! And what? You're gonna hold them for the police? You know? And I mean I'd been all in favor of them getting their ass kicked. Because you don't do that, you know? You don't like what we do? Don't fuck with them then. You do your thing, but don't be blocking, holding somebody. But I think those are some of the things that we're gonna have to deal with as different movements.

I always say that there is going to be again at some point, beyond me, I ain't gotta be a part of it, a Black Liberation Army, you know? At this point there is effectively no Black Liberation Army in a physical sense. But, because you've got people like me and Assata who have given the story, the Black Liberation Army exists in the minds of a whole lot of young people out there. You hear it in their hip hop, in their writings, and them making other kinds of forms of communication. At some point, there are gonna be those who get together and say "we gotta take it to the next place," you know? And then you're going to see where others in the movement place themselves, in relation to that, you know? How many people was supporting Assata when Assata Shakur first got captured? Was only a few, you know? White movement in general? no. Weather Underground? Yes. Black Nationalist Groups? Yes. You know? When she got liberated, same thing. It was like some people still had the nerve to criticize her. But we were just like OK, listen, we gonna get our political prisoners out by any means necessary. That's it. If you don't know why, try to consider what our lives is like in your position, in relation to us. Don't put your moral standards on us, don't do none of that stuff, we are fighting for our very lives. It is really war on us, you know? And if people can't recognize that we ain't got time to get into the debates and all the other stuff. And believe me it's not romantic to take a position of armed struggle, it's not romantic to go underground, it's not romantic to see your comrade get shot, die right in front of you. That stuff is not romantic. What drives us to that point, where we feel we gotta take this system on, take the war to them, you know? It ain't just like frustration and we're just irrational. We have thought about it. We have felt it. We have waited. You think about the fact that you ain't never going to see your family again, but it's for your family. You think about the fact that you wanna see your children grow up, but you know that your life might end in the next six months or next year, whatever. You might go to prison. And a lot of us, you know, I mean a lot of us felt like, 20? We was either gonna be dead or in prison, you know, but we gonna give it our best shot.

Abolition as Zapatismo

Xican@patistas Autonomxs

The following are our perspectives as organizers on the ground, working in the borderlands in occupied Kumeyaay Territory. Here we draw on work with an organization that listens to and accompanies asylum seekers and migrants detained in a modern-day concentration camp: the Otay Mesa Detention Center (OMDC) *alongside increasing calls to abolish ICE, the police, and all borders*. The preliminary analysis provided here is our attempt to outline what abolition can look like when joined to a praxis of Zapatismo.

For starters, we take abolition to mean the collective liberation of our communities. It is the imagining and creation of autonomous spaces where we can exist in dignified ways and in actual community with one another. This is opposed to the forms of competition to which capitalism drives individuals and communities as a whole.

What we mean by Zapatismo as praxis are the seven Zapatista principles that guide our organizing: to obey, not command; to serve others, not serve oneself; to build, not destroy; to propose, not impose; to represent, not supplant; to convince, not defeat; to go below, not above. Abolition thus becomes the process of creating that autonomous space, not

Abolition thus becomes the process of creating that autonomous space, not individually or abstractly, but through a set of practices of collectivity and conviviality.

individually or abstractly, but through a set of practices of collectivity and conviviality. In order for abolition to take hold, to grow within and without the *entrañas* (entrails) of what the Zapatistas have called the capitalist hydra, there thus needs to be an organizational praxis with a logic that exists outside of, or at minimum works to evade, the logic of racial capitalism.

We hold that the capitalist hydra, or racial capitalism, is best understood as a civilization of death, as a world economic system that exploits and controls much of the resources in the world, with only a few benefiting, by feeding on real and imagined social divisions. Nevertheless, the reality is that there is a much larger world that has existed outside this logic, that continues to exist and resist in a variety of forms. That world is known by many names: Indigenous communities that are currently resisting and have resisted for centuries. Indeed, there are more people outside the logic of said civilizational impulse whose lives are not guided by a profit motive, but one of conviviality with one another while honoring and protecting land and life. These are not abstract idealizations, but rather, the current water defenders and land defenders of our times.

What makes the Zapatista communities, in particular, such a globally recognized and influential movement that has inspired many more movements is that they actively seek to operate outside the logic of capitalism and have proven to the world that it is possible to do so in order to create a world where many worlds fit. As such, it is up to us in our respective communities or *trincheras* (trenches) to resist and live dignified lives by creating not two, three, or many Vietnams, but more and more *caracoles*, more sustainable, equitable lives that allow from our *trincheras* the flourishing of new ways of living and ultimately new worlds.

Abolition is the *Ya Basta!* of today. It means: Stop dehumanizing peoples and communities! Stop destroying the natural world! STOP with the system that is against life itself!!! *Ya Basta!* Enough! Abolish the state, the police, ICE, borders!! These are all institutions that cannot be reformed under the logic of capitalism; they need to be abolished, destroyed.

Abolition has inspired the imagination, just like the Zapatistas, in terms of what it would mean to have a world without prisons, without detention centers, police, or ICE. For the first time, abolition is in the mainstream media, and discussion in communities on how to abolish the police or cut police resources is happening in many cities across the U.S. For the first time, there is more visibility from the perspective of the people documenting their truths and exposing the continued violence at the hands of police.

There have been many George Floyds, and the promise is that there will not be another George Floyd forgotten with impunity. The world will know what has happened to the countless Black and Brown lives as we continue to make our case for abolition. George Jackson long ago argued that if we need one word to describe the coming fascist time, that word would be reform. The time of reform is over. Welcome to a new wave of continued struggle for justice, for actual transformation, and true abolition. Welcome to the world of global and intercommunal Zapatismo!

To understand abolition today, it is important to understand the historical context of the abolition movement in the 19th century and its quest for the liberation of enslaved Black people in the white-supremacist, settler-colonial entity called the United States. The passage and ratification of the 13th Amendment to the U.S. Constitution in 1865, simply reformed the racist institution of slavery as it allowed for an exception clause to its presumed outlawing. Said loophole prohibited slavery and indentured

To understand abolition today, it is important to understand the historical context of the abolition movement in the 19th century and its quest for the liberation of enslaved Black people in the white supremacist, settler colonial entity called the United States.

servitude "except as a punishment for crime whereof the party shall have been duly convicted," paving the way for the convict lease system that allowed for prison labor to be contracted out to private interests for profit, oftentimes to the very same previous slaveowners. This practice, while rooted in the continued exploitation of African Americans after the Civil War, paved the way for other forms of captive labor of communities deemed expendable for the color of their skin, in turn also exploiting their labor, creating a second class of poor people: working-class migrant laborers not seen as worthy of citizenship.

Earlier forms of captive labor have been compounded by the detention and warehousing of would-be migrants, refugees, and asylum seekers towards similar ends. While the series of narratives, from the formerly enslaved to the Chinese, Japanese, Irish, and Italians, may differ in the details, as does the captivity of Indigenous children sent to boarding schools or the detribalization of Mexican laborers, the end result coheres in a structure of racial capitalism that divides and exploits through dehumanization all the same. Moreover, we see this logic in the blocking of migration from countries where racial capitalism has already destroyed their means of sustainability, as well as from Muslim countries, and more recently Haitian and African countries because of Title 42.

What is currently happening is the structures of capitalism are proving themselves unsustainable. Wealthier states are continuing to build and enforce their borders, causing more violence and death to those making their trajectory to the centers of capital. The Zapatistas refer to this time as the storm; the walls of capitalism will continue to be built and become more bloody, resources will be plundered, and there will be more scarcity around the world. Capitalism cannot fix the destruction and hole it has created for itself, and the only way to not face the reality of its destruction is to cage itself from the problems and chaos of the world. The Zapatistas' analysis of the storm is not unlike Aime Cesaire's declaration that a civilization that is unable to solve the problems it creates is a decadent civilization, a dying civilization. The question is: How can we bring forth the death of a civilization of death?

This capitalist system is no longer being sustained by the imperialist and neoliberal forms that had sought to fix previous economic crises. Thus, the fundamental political dilemma that needs to be addressed is the need to dismantle this entire civilization that is anything but civil; all of its institutions of power that thrive on profit, death and destruction—from universities, social welfare, and the criminal justice system to financial institutions and healthcare systems. We need to do more than abolish ICE, more than abolish the police, and more than abolish borders; those are simply the bonds or glue that hold together the assemblage of states and

> The question is: How can we bring forth the death of a civilization of death?

institutions as a unified civilizational whole.
It is not about saving what is good or not
good about the civilization of death. It means
that everything this system is dependent on
is premised upon and sustains itself through
the social fabric of racial capitalism, and it
will continue to surveil, police, and consume
all aspects of our lives until it is destroyed.
But that "until" is key because it speaks to the
radical hope we need, one that must take root
in our ancestral and Indigenous knowledges
and practices, in the defense of our territories
and those of the peoples of where we reside,
and in the honoring of land and life. And at
the same time, it must take root in the new
imaginaries to be built collectively in our
respective communities.

The border
"crisis" is not
about a broken
immigration
system or a
broken asylum
system;

the crisis is the
existence of
borders.

Case in point: the border "crisis" is
not about a broken immigration system or
a broken asylum system; the crisis is the
existence of borders. These systems are doing
exactly what they are intended to do: to
continue to oppress Black and Brown bodies
and peoples for profit because they/we, will
never be seen as human beings as long as we
live in a white-supremacist world. We agree,
there are many fronts to fight the ongoing
problems that result from displacement,
Indigenous dispossession, and continued
abuses by Customs and Border Protection
(CBP), police, and border patrol. We must
not be naive; yes legal help, legislative help,
humanitarian help may alleviate some issues,
but they are not sufficient so long as we

continue to live under a racial capitalist logic.

The U.S. Empire only serves to create an artificial sense of national identity and false illusion of prosperity, hope, and justice. It has no real interest in the reality of how millions of people are living, being displaced from their homelands, militarized through war, living under extreme poverty, with no food or water to continue to feed and support their families. It instead feeds itself off such misery. Its institutional apparatuses—CBP, police, border patrol, and others—mark migrants, refugees, Black and Brown bodies and peoples, as less than human, and one way it legitimizes itself is by making claims that people need to do the so-called "right thing" of waiting in an imaginary legal line as the only way of getting legal citizenship or having an asylum claim accepted.

These crises at the border will continue to persist so long as we feed the frenzy of multinational corporations under a globalized capitalism. How do we respond, organize, and mobilize? There is no one answer or one way. All approaches that help bring visibility to the problem matter, but some end up leaving long-term problems for others to resolve. Or worse yet, they re-inscribe national imaginaries when the problem is ultimately global in nature.

When it comes to the idea of abolishing the border, we thus recognize that, in most immigrant rights work, at times seems as if we are just putting a bandage on top of another bandage. Helping support one family or one person is, indeed, a small victory in itself, but it can be a drain of energy that affects the psyche. Nevertheless, all politics is local. This is the *trinchera*, or trench, in which we find ourselves while never losing sight of the various tentacles of Empire.

Some decades back, Linda Bosniak warned that to engage in migrants' rights work while not challenging the very existence of borders at the same time is itself contradictory; by accepting national borders, one is inadvertently committed to the condition of possibility that creates vulnerabilities for migrant, refugee, and asylum seekers. Thus, the problem we are facing requires more than international solidarity, which maintains borders in place.

Instead, our language needs to change to articulate our enemy as not

We are not here to center anyone's one struggle, for "there is no center, there is no periphery" those are only the cartographies of power that we seek to transform rather than invert.

just a broken national immigration system that isn't living up to the (false) promise of freedom and opportunity, but rather, we need to name U.S. Empire, global racial capitalism, colonialism, hetero-patriarchy, and the continued oppression that touch all of us on a global scale. It also means our forms of networking and organization must also change. We recognize there are processes and institutions of captivity and enclosure worldwide (e.g., mass incarceration, detention centers, forced labor, among others) locking away millions of People of Color, poor people, Indigenous communities, queer siblings, women, Black and Brown bodies for the benefit of extracting their labor and whatever forms of value can be used to benefit multinational corporations. These forms of captive labor help sustain global systemic racism and global white supremacy that privileges the white bodies of the world. The Otay Mesa Detention Center (OMDC) is but one microcosm of the problem that we find before us.

We do not claim to have a blueprint on how to abolish detention centers, prisons, borders, state powers. Yet we hope that what we do at OMDC, and how we do it through accompaniment, can inspire others to organize themselves. We are not here to center anyone's one struggle, for "there is no center, there is no periphery"–those are only the cartographies of power that we seek to transform rather than invert. We are here to accompany each other's struggles as we do the work of abolition starting in our local context.

We organize and accompany detainee *compas* around their decisions to organize: how to and when to organize because we understand they are the ones at the front line of that particular *trinchera*. We do not impose our agenda or present ourselves as if we know best. Many on the inside have no idea what abolition is and do not care to. They are just concerned about their personal freedom and their loved ones. The discrimination and homophobia experienced at the hands of officers, and at times even amongst *compas* themselves, is felt as strongly as the systemic oppression across various axes of domination that is reproduced in the continued abuses inside and outside detention centers and prisons. This is but a glimpse of what is shared to us by the *compas* through hotlines we help operate.

Therefore, we recognize there is no way of knowing how to organize until we start to organize together in struggle. We do this by doing and learning as we do. What is key is that the approaches and the strategies must be derived from collective work. The approach our organizational work has taken has been to understand the long-term global problem and know that this fight is not going to be won overnight but instead requires a long-term approach of accompaniment with our incarcerated and detained siblings until all borders, detention centers, prisons, and capitalism have fallen. We are in

We are in accompaniment because we ourselves are not safe and because we ourselves are not outside this problem;

we are in accompaniment because we ourselves are also in struggle.

accompaniment because we ourselves are not safe and because we ourselves are not outside this problem; we are in accompaniment because we ourselves are also in struggle, battling police brutality, systemic racism in all sectors of society and levels of government. We fight for the preservation of our natural resources, our water, land, and the integrity of Indigenous communities.

We are in accompaniment because we choose not just solidarity; we ourselves chose to resist. We do not agree with conceptions of ally-ship as a political framework, because our Zapatismo is personal; it is about commiting our entire lives fighting for liberation. We do not proclaim ourselves to support poor oppressed communities who we recognize as different from ourselves. Ours is not a temporary strategic approach to be allies in distinct struggles, to show we are down for your cause, or that you are down with our cause. In such a framing, both remain separate causes, and we remain siloed communities with other borders between us.

Ours is not about individualizing approaches of shaming white fragility and other fragilities or about taking stock of each other's privileges, as if oppression can be resolved through a scorecard. While we recognize power relations continue to mark all of us, we choose not to frame our political praxis in terms of the internal fissures and divides among or towards each other, or reduce our differences to a sameness. On the

> We are in accompaniment because we choose not just solidarity;
>
> we ourselves chose to resist.

contrary, as the Zapatistas remind us, we are equal because we are different.

Life is precious and we must live as communities, see each other in community, and survive together guided by intercommunal and intergenerational commitments of reciprocity. We do this by arriving at one collective agreement at a time, and by organizing carefully and strategically as if our lives depended on it. Taking the seven principles of Zapatismo seriously in every collective decision we make has been a way to both unlearn the logics of capital that seek to divide and exploit us, and to begin to learn a new way of thinking, feeling, walking, and being in the world not just for ourselves but for our various others as a starting point for our own liberation. We bring on the death of a civilization of death through an affirmation of life itself!

Sunset Park, 2040

Gisselle Jiménez, Jess Kulig, Corbin Laedlein, and Michelle Yun
Sunset Park Popular Assembly

It's been 15 years since The Uprising. Members of the Sunset Park Popular Assembly reflect on daily life in a liberated East Lenapehoking and how they each contribute to their community.

////

San, age 20:

My day began early, harvesting pumpkins in the *milpa* that surrounds Sunset Park. In between poking around the prickly leaves and vines for ripe pumpkins, I'd watch my neighbors go about their morning routines. I spotted my *compa* Valerie from the Youth Council passing by on 5th Avenue and waved. "Buenos días, San!" she called from the street, "See you tonight!"

Working at the *milpa* can be hard work, but I enjoy this rotation of my Urban Agroecology apprenticeship more than the oyster and seaweed cooperative at Jamel Floyd Park—I'll take scratchy vines over the freezing water any day. Most of what's produced by the farm cooperatives gets distributed to local schools, and it feels good knowing that my work contributes to my community's health and autonomy.

At the *milpa* I work with Auntie Joanne (who can be found with her famous homemade cookies and cosmetics at the Thursday Night Market) and Don Rigoberto (who's never caught without his signature embroidered vest) from the *Sindicato de Campesines Urbanes*. They can talk a lot, but they are also great listeners and so kind—they always make sure to feed me after a morning of hard work. Today, Don Rigo brought tamales made from our own corn, and Auntie Jo brought scallion pancakes.

We sat in the orchard for lunch after the harvest. Auntie Jo and Don Rigo talked of how it was before the Popular Assemblies instituted land reform; how our Mother Earth and homes were called "property" and "real estate"; how landlords bought and sold them for profit, forcing the dispossessed and racialized peoples to rent tiny crumbling apartments or live in the streets, public parks, and subways; of how the *malgobierno* and the political parties ruled from above, serving the interests of the landlords and bosses while they manipulated our people with false promises and fear.

Everything we could see—from the *milpa*, to my apartment building, to the salt marshes of Manahatta in the distance—had been collectivized and redistributed according to social and ecological need following The Uprising. The original stewards of this territory, the Lenape, had rematriated back

I listened as I ate, feeling humbled and grateful to those who sacrificed to free the Earth and her people, allowing us, as Don Rigo says, "to finally be human beings again."

to their homeland after the fall of the colonial government, and now all decisions over land-use here in East Lenapehoking are made with their consultation and consent.

From where we sat, I could see the memorial to those martyred by the *malgobierno's* police, *migra*, and military in the northeast corner of the park. I stared at it as Auntie Jo shared that there were times when she almost lost hope, when fascism seemed inevitable. A truck with a loudspeaker went up 44th Street, reminding us that our neighborhood assembly was this evening. I listened as I ate, feeling humbled and grateful to those who sacrificed to free the Earth and her people, allowing us, as Don Rigo says, "to finally be human beings again."

////

J, age 43:

Hiba, Sofía, and Celeste all stayed home from school today. Everyone's exhausted from the fun last night, so we decided to sleep in. Hiba's aunt and cousin—Amti Souad and Basma—are leaving to go back to Morocco on Saturday, and Frankie just got back from San Francisco de Macorís, so we celebrated with food and karaoke in Sunset Park. Hiba spent a lot of time learning to cook with her aunt this past month, so she made couscous for everyone. It was delicious—especially with all the vegetables from the *milpa*. Frankie had everyone rolling on the ground laughing with her throwback Disney covers. Sofía, of course, was so happy to see her again. Her connection with Frankie is special.

Frankie and I were the first ones up this morning, so the two of us walked over to see our friends on 54th Street. Shaun and some of the *tíos* from the block made a huge batch of his famous chicken and waffles, so we picked up enough for all of us. Frances gave us some maple syrup that she tapped in the Bronx, and I had a bottle of hot sauce left from my visit to my sister, the perfect touches for the meal.

Over breakfast, the kids asked us to tell them stories about when we were children. It's always fascinating to see their reactions. Even though it hasn't been that long, their world is so different. Today, I told them about the time I got my hair cut short for the first time. I loved how my new haircut looked on me, but when I went to school, the kids all laughed at me. One of the teachers even scolded me when I went to the bathroom, telling me, "This is the *girls'* restroom." I tried to explain how stressful it was, but Sofía and Celeste just giggled. They thought it was so silly that my short hair was such a big deal!

Amti Souad chimed in, "You think that's strange? 15 years ago we couldn't even come here without permission from the government! We tried for years and years, but they just wouldn't give us that damn piece of paper! They rarely gave them to people like us..." The kids twisted their faces, perplexed. They've heard about borders and visas and citizenship before, since many of our friends, family, and neighbors have stories—stories about living in the shadows; stories about being separated from loved ones by invisible lines in the sand; stories about crossing those lines, only to suffer exploitation and oppression on the other side; and stories of being placed inside dark, cold cells. But they still don't totally understand. I don't think I would either. People have freedom to move around now, and no longer have to fear being thrown into a cold, dark cell by the government.

The kids finished breakfast and got ready to meet their friends at Jamel Floyd Park, close to the site where the infamous MDC prison once stood. Sometimes I feel jealous of them— jealous that they never had to go up against the

Even though it hasn't been that long, their world is so different.

big land developers who wanted to force us all out of the neighborhood, or that they'll never have to worry about their loved ones being locked behind those drab walls at MDC. But I'm also grateful for how we've been able to transform Sunset Park since The Uprising, and I'm excited to see what we can continue to make of this world together. And I can't lie; I do love seeing the elders' faces every time Celeste confuses the word "landlord" for "wizard!"

////

Esperanza, age 84

My morning *cafecito* tastes better by the window. My neighbors wave to me as they trickle down our block on their way to work at the waterfront. Saleem, Krystal, Jin Hui, Xiomara, AJ... a knock at the door. I finish the last sip of coffee and grab my cane to answer. "*Áo zǎo*, Señora Esperanza!" Jenni greets me with a big smile. "I picked an eggplant for you along with some more pigeon pea pods ready for shelling. I'm running late for my apprenticeship at the bike shop so I'll catch you at our meeting later!" She takes off before I can thank her.

For the last few years, Jenni has tended my plot on our building's shared rooftop *conuco*. It's my piece of the Taíno Nation here in Lenapehoking. I miss the thick, humid air of the greenhouse, but I can't make the climb up to the roof anymore. Here on the ground I still have our native plant garden, the blooming tree my mother left me, and the community that grows in its shade. I lean out the window and ask one of the neighborhood children running up the hill to PS94 to stop and pass me a fistful of bee balm from the garden.

Unmarried and without children, I never imagined I'd have anyone to leave anything to. When the pandemic struck, I was at risk and alone. Soon young folks from the Popular Assembly noticed my solitude and began to bring me groceries and sometimes, from a safe distance, they'd linger to learn more about me. They resurfaced memories of my childhood in the mountains of Kiskeya where all we had was each other, the river, and God. It was humble but we had dignity. I stir my pot of *sancocho* and watch the steam rise to fill the room with the smell of my island.

In the years leading to The Uprising, those young people reminded me our city was made of *islas* too, and that we lived on earth and among rivers that could still sustain us and teach us and heal us, if only we cared for the land in return. They reminded me we still had each other, and that we needed each other. They said they needed even me. I'd been alone for so long I had forgotten what that felt like. How could I have known my stories would be fuel for a revolution? How could my mother have known my name, Esperanza, would be prophetic?

Now I serve with the Elders Council of the Popular Assembly, guided by Lenape elders to revive and preserve the knowledge that took generations to accumulate. This month, we on the Safety Committee prepared a discussion series on peacemaking and restorative justice practices in other communities in order to continue developing our own practices in Sunset Park. Tonight we'll study the Mamas of Rojava, a group of women elders in liberated Syria who have kept their community safe by serving as mediators between the families they already know and love.

As the late afternoon sun begins to tinge everything gold, Jenni, AJ, Xiomara, Jin Hui, Krystal, and Saleem drag themselves back up the steep hill of our block and plop down heavily in our garden like overripe fruit. I carefully bring a tall pitcher of iced bee balm

> How could I have known my stories would be fuel for a revolution?

tea to the window sill and sweeten it with honey from the *milpa's* apiary. I give them time to fill their bottles with the pale pink drink and rest in the breeze under my mother's tree before we begin our meeting. I pour myself a glass last. Everything tastes better by the window.

Glossary

Áo zǎo   good morning [Fujian/Min Chinese]

Cafecito   coffee

Compa   short for compañera/compañero/compañerx, meaning companion or comrade

Conuco   a Taíno word for an area used for the cultivation of vegetables, fruits, staple crops and medicine, which was foundational to the pre colonial agriculture systems throughout the Caribbean.

El Mal Gobierno   "the bad government;" a term popularized by the Zapatistas to refer to the dominant government/political system that rules from above to serve capitalism and the civilization of death.

Islas   islands

Kiskeya   the indigenous name for the island that today is home to Haiti and the Dominican Republic.

Migra   immigration police (slang)

Milpa   traditional farming system practiced throughout Mesoamerica, often including corn, beans, and squash. Derived from Nahuatl, meaning "cultivated field."

Sancocho   A stew/soup found throughout the Caribbean that traditionally consists of meat, tubers, and vegetables served in a broth.

Sindicato de campesines urbanes   Union of Urban Peasant Farmers

Tío   uncle

Mandar Obedeciendo
from an Urban Xicano's World
in Seven *Travesías* on Tovaangnar/L.A.

Kristian E. Vazquez

Desde la selva urbana
The city of angels is weeping.
Its smog-filled air fills
a skyline of towering pillars,
bleeding onto its rows of households,
stretching far and wide,
communities cut through
by the freeway circuits
of free-flowing automobiles,
pumping the blood of the weeping heart,
a heart torn from the Tongva people.

What of this city and its rails?
A movement of bodies, people,
cultures suspended in a jurisdiction
of killer cops, killer jails,
killer detention centers...
The screams of its people
are inexhaustible,
clouded by the exhausts of my
metro bus line on my way to school,
inhibiting the Brown and Black workers
surviving the world of Capital
surviving the world of *la hidra*

Servir y no servirse.
The lies the schools teach us
are the same lies from 1492.
500 years of constant struggle
against the scaffolding of history
books sent to tame me, us, we.
What does this knowledge serve
if not the master's house?
Remember the siege:
Mexican American studies, banned.
Ethnic Studies, banned.
Burned books of deep,
precious knowledge,
Banned from the hands of
Raza youth,
Banned from the hands of
Raza teachers,
Banned from the hands of
a community.
But what are the master's tools
if not the books
that tell us we are foreigners?

Lies serve no one
but those from above.
How do we serve our
People?
How do we serve our
Pueblo?
How do we know what we know
in our Autonomous hearts?
We don't serve no masters,
We obey a purpose
Or perhaps a feeling
That we will be free.
We serve the people,
The people we serve,
We,
The people,
Without masters
Only us.

Representar y no suplantar.
I remember the echo
Of a distant land,
Lands that conquer
Lands that bleed
Lands that weep
Lands that coerce the body
Those too were my lands
My people
My ancestors
Myself
Suspended by law,
by authority
by a voice commanding
telling us nothing but orders

Representing no one
But a force of domination.
Our bodies touch that
Ancient code—
a whisper of a collective
Heart—
A reason to speak
A method to move
Together and not
Without
We are we
We speak as one
We move as one
We know together
We feel freedom

Construir y no destruir.
My families converge on this dirt
These territories of rivers, mountains,
Deserts,
These villages of an Uto-Aztecan tongue
These warrior hunters,
These people who emerged
With acorn trees
With nuts, berries, and trading flows.
My families are distant relatives
Un-becoming on their own roads
To find home here
In these modern metropoles
With their suburban terrors
And their divided lines of race.
What is a Tongva turned Chicano?
What is a Chicano turned Indian?
My families diverge here

Fragmented by de-industrial ruins
Destroyed by Capital, by profits.
I grew up here tasting the bitter
Mexican life of slow death
knowing I desired life.
Today I see a new convergence
From below and with the land
Sowing life of seeds and laughter
Between Tongva and Chicano
Between Native and migrant
Between life and death
I see another world in motion.

Obedecer y no mandar.
Zapatismo existe en Los Angeles
Una excursión por la vida
Tiembla de la tierra de hormigón
Tearing apart the bureaucrats
Toppling brick buildings
Filling potholes in poor hoods
Building from love
Accepting no defeat
Threading a weave of struggle
Contra los patrones de lucha
Más allá del autoridad
Listening to the elders
Hearing the children
Following the youth
I have seen the land of
Mandar Obedeciendo
Flowering like a stalk of *maíz*
Or buried like a *papa* waiting to
See the light of the sky
Cultivated by a caring soil

Where the darkness sows life
Loving waters
Blessed by the sacred Sun
No one person here has *la manda*
We obey the people

Proponer y no imponer.
In the City of Angels
Lives a world of overlapping universes
A cosmic rift in cosmopolitanism
A city-state of authoritarian magnitude
Where the below lives in crisis
Where the imposition of city codes
And police
Haunt the lives of migrants
Black people
Poor neighborhoods
Hoods defending themselves
From white or other investors
From corporate agendas
Gentrification
All while Los Angeles dictates its boundaries
Its limits
Its threshold
I myself an imposter
Living unincorporated
Deep in the streets of South Gate
Another jurisdiction of imposed laws
Without process of the voice of the below
How do we enable another proposal?
A proposal for life?
A proposal for another kind of
Urbanism?

Convencer y no vencer.
I have seen the tensions between
Anarchists
Maoists
Zapatistas
Here on the lands of Tovaangnar
The conflicts between
Mexicans
Central Americans
Black people
Indigenous Tongva
Migrants
Undocumented
Whites
Rich
Poor
People of Color
Authentic
Appropriator
I have seen the refusals
Of organized collective action
Only the embracing of solidarity
In the trenches of spontaneous rebellions
To convince the people is to do away
With our critiques of defeat
We hold in our hands
The assembly
The rallies
The marches
But do we hold in our hearts
The capacity to listen?

Bajar y no subir.
Through the streets of Silver Lake
We once encountered a bolt of energy
Filling the streets with lowriders and
Chicanx families holding it down
Playing those smooth oldies from
Loudspeakers;
We too cruised to see the below
In action
In commemoration
To yell loud from a Chicanx vernacular
"We too are still here"
Bumping sounds in the night
Showing in vibrant colored cars
The voice of expressive machines
Those delicate metal vehicles
Bouncing up and down
With kids racing on their bicycles
Catching the below's desires
From the edges of their video-phones;
It's the everyday people
Like my own family
That we must enter through
To assemble a different kind of movement
Something the Zapatistas call
A Journey for Life
And our journey is in the urban jungles
Of Los Angeles;
Our autonomy is from our hearts too.

U.S. from Below and to the Left Encounters *Tierra Insumisa*: Fragments, Dreams, and Notes

Kristian E. Vasquez, Maritza Geronimo,
Gustavo García, and Natalia Toscano

Between August 9 and 19 of 2021, members of Sexta Grietas del Norte converged on Madrid, Spain to accompany the Zapatista voyage to a very other Europe, a Europe "from below and to the left." Our report back documents our witnessing and encountering of the people of that land the Zapatistas have come to rename Slumil K'ajxemk'op, Tierra Insumisa, *Insubmissive Land.*

* * *

from Kristian E. Vasquez

I woke up a bit disoriented. As my circadian rhythm was adjusting to the time/space I arrived to, I realized myself—a Xicano—on the lands of another Europe, another Spain that I only knew from a colonial history narrated to me in Chicanx Studies classes, a reality that lived in my genetic code and on the surface of my largest organ, my skin. I woke up to a Spain from below and to the left that was full of a history of communists, anarchists, feminists, and other radicals that held Zapatismo to the level of a political philosophy or a set of practices that opposed capitalism, colonialism, and patriarchy—in Madrid, I woke to a city that spoke *castellano* but also spoke rebellion. Only having been here for a few days, the group I traveled with—the *compas* from our collective project Chicanx World-Making & Futurities—were encountering Madrid for the first time—alongside our *compas* from Sexta networks and the Zapatista journalist world.

We were here as neither tourists nor as researchers—we were here to witness and learn how Spain from below, *España del abajo*, resisted. We accompanied the *mesas de trabajo*, encounters, workshops, and mobilizations of organized resistance from below that was led by various groups and collectives. In encountering Spain from below, we listened to the people who resisted here and who were building another world in rebellion, surging to become a world of many worlds—we witnessed a new becoming that was initiated by the *Esquadrón 421*, a contingent of seven Zapatistas who traveled by boat to Europe.

Here I share a few reflections, quotes, notes, and musings from *Tierra Insumisa*, another Europe from below re-named by the Zapatistas on their Journey for Life; it means a land that does not submit to domination "insubmissive land." I share this spirit of rebellious lands as I journeyed here to *Tierra Insumisa* to learn from these lands a rebellious spirit and activity that desired self-organization and autonomy, life and joy, land and liberation.

*   *   *

from Kristian E. Vasquez

Today, August 13, 2021, is five-hundred years since the fall of Mexico-Tenochtitlan, the city-temple-state located in the central valley of what is today Ciudad de México, México. Making part of the Triple Alliance, the fall Mexico-Tenochtitlan symbolized a day of ceded power, an emergence of colonial domination by way of conquest. Yet, as the Zapatistas and many *pueblos indígenas* tell us all around the world, we/they were never conquered.

On the geographies of Spain, on the Gregorian calendar of time, and in the mode of resistance by way of encounters and building relations, the groups who are accompanying and hosting *Esquadrón 421* welcomed us, a small group from *El Otro Estados Unidos*, the Other United States, with open arms, curious questions, and mystical theories of how we resisted from below and to the left in a world-imperialist power that constituted the Global North.

For many of us in Mexican, Mexican-American, Chicanx, Latinx communities, or American Indian territories from the U.S. Southwest, we understand Spain to be a contemporary nation-state that historically colonized large geographies of *Las Américas*—or how the Kuna *pueblos* call it, *Abya Yala*. For us, the Judeo-Christian kingdom of Castile and Aragón that would conquer the Iberian Peninsula in January 1492 and become the Spanish Crown/Monarchy that would invade central *Anahuac* in 1521 lives on as a colonial consciousness of who we are as people historically constituted by colonial domination. I am here to say that Spain as a nation-state today is an oppressive entity, but the people themselves are not our enemies.

Los pueblos aquí en España estan en resistencia. They are not a homogenous, monolithic, or single group of people that seek violence on us as people of *Las Américas*. They, too, are in rebellion, in struggle, and are building another world from below and to the left.

In the narrations and *comunicados* of *las (comunidades)* y *los (pueblos)* Zapatistas, this day we yell, *¡no nos conquistaron!* Five-hundred years means more than a colonial history; it is a story of resistance, of struggle, and it is beyond only us—it is a struggle for the whole planet that seeks life, that desires another way to live outside and beyond capital's hold on our lives. We resist the narrative that we are conquered by capitalism, that there is no other alternative.

* * *

from Maritza Geronimo

The name *Tierra Insumisa* was given to the European geographies and people. A renaming of the land that uplifts the rebellions from below in these territories and is also a call to create a new geography, a new way of relating to the land, and each other.

Yesterday a man in a *circulo de trabajo* said *"la tierra insumisa se tiene que crear"* (we have to build this rebellious land). It was a given name but it must be continuously put into practice and built together.

The *compas* from Europe say the tour has allowed them to *conocernos* (get to know each other) and from across the sea we also came to *conocer*. To learn about a place our bodies and minds are forever linked to, but I never thought as a *Xicana Indígena* that I would be here. Two geographies and world views colliding once again. The *compas* from Spain don't seem to sit with the legacies of colonialism in the same ways as we do. I have not heard them mention colonization of the Americas or the ways it has changed or impacted their lives. Yet I sit in these spaces with them and have moments of bodily remembrance, a temporal and spatial rift, and I am transported back to 1492. I feel enraged, confused, lost. What am I doing in Spain? What am I doing sitting here in circle with *les conquistadores*? My body and mind return to the present. Colonization sits heaving in my heart and mind as it is everywhere in this city, on every street name and building. The legacies of colonialism never ended for us in the Americas, and it never ended here in Madrid either. So what now? What do we do in this new moment of convergence?

—August 13, 2021, 12:14pm

* * *

from Kristian E. Vasquez

For many of us, Chicanxs or Xican@s, La Chicanada or La Xicanada, we hold in our spirit a different kind of reality in the United States, one that narrates resistance and rebellion of another kind of space, a middle space, that articulates struggle for another kind of being, knowledge, feeling, and existence.

We walk the path of Chicanismo or Xicanism@ or whatever we want to call it. We have named ourselves, who we belong to, who we walk with, and who we build with. We named ourselves to resist a naming by the Anglo State, by that apparatus that absorbs and assimilates *La Raza*, or in other words, people not part of the dreams and fantasies of the Anglo world. In our mistakes we still walk. In our errors we still struggle. In the face of death, violence, and destruction, we still live and breathe. In the face of rhetorical extinction, we live on unbothered. We are neither race nor nation. We are a movement of people, of a group of groups that don't always agree with each other. We walk so that we may live.

The introduction of Zapatismo into our orbit of thought, action, and doing has forever re-shaped us since the global mobilizations and organized resistance of 1968 to the migrant justice movements of the 1990s against fascist policies to deport undocumented communities. We are not rigid as many perceive us to be—we constitute a work-in-progress as we continuously re-build our path, *nuestres caminos*.

We accompany the Zapatistas not out of isolated solidarity but because we share a common struggle: to liberate ourselves from capital's death-drive, to build autonomous life.

*   *   *

from Gustavo García

"La gira por la vida"
1492
Still fresh in our minds
500 years later
la gira por la vida
urges for a collaboration
a unity
a willing to learn
for those
who believe in the many visions
of new relationalities
possibilities,
and worldmaking
those who believe in the power
of the people
who are and continue to be
below and to the left

we
los pueblos originarios
are still here,
we never left,
we moved around,
fought back,
navigated colonial conditions,
capitalist structures,
heteropatriarchal logics and practices

500 years later
la gira por la vida
makes the call,
teleport, transport, and organize
learn,
connect,
build,
communicate,
believe in each other,
And most importantly
love one another

we
have a duty
a commitment
a *cargo*
a responsibility
say the Zapatistas, CNI, CIG
travel and follow the *gira*
go to the places where you least expect
particularly the geographies that remind us of
the pain
Spain, Germany, France, Portugal
a psyche and way of being imprinted in our
mind

yet distant, unfamiliar, and full of mysteries
meet, connect, and organize with people from
from below and the left
what are their stories?
what are their struggles?
what is our responsibility?

our struggle in the continent
of *las Americas*
started 500 years ago
1492
1492
1492
colonial imposition and occupation
the islands,
mainlands,
and continent
moments and stories passed down
experiences we continue to live
marked on our flesh
in our being
in our essence
in our future

La Gira Por la Vida
Una llamada of what must happen,
the building of collective visions
of global relations
of decolonial possibilities
a recognition of struggle
a recognition of beauty
a recognition of love
a recognition of learning
a recognition of subversive practices

a practice of radical relationality
a practice of communal governance
a practice of respect and honor
a building of collective futures

thank you, *gracias, shushchirluu*
Desde las trincheras donde se comen tlayudas
y se mantiene la rebeldía

* * *

from Kristian E. Vasquez

I look toward new politics, or perhaps an anti-politics, that re-considers the modes of resistances that ground our work for a radical transformation of our societies that operate from a desire to dominate with a brutal reprise for power. How do we build together? How do we get free?

The fall of Mexico-Tenochtitlan on August 13 five-hundred years ago is more than how we understand the narrations of Mexica-Tenochca stories after supposed conquest. It is a symbolic date that operates as way for us to re-locate ourselves, our struggles, and how we understand time. From the *barrios de España*, the fall of Mexico-Tenochtitlan is the resurgence of struggle for life.

* * *

from Natalia Toscano

The journey to Madrid has been riddled with emotions of uncertainty, curiosity, and determination. I never imagined visiting Europe, much less Spain, as my resentment towards the state has been embedded in my being. Despite these sentiments, I aimed to come with an open mind and open heart to listen and learn from the *compas*. Sharing memories and stories, the *compas* from *La Otra Europa* have offered alternative windows to this world that for so long has occupied a place of privilege in my imaginary. Here, with *Europa Insumisa*, I've learned about their feminist, anti-racist, and immigrant struggles. We've had glimpses to the class struggles and anti-fascist struggles in Spain, France, and Germany. The Zapatistas in their *Gira por La Vida* have created an opportunity to weave ourselves together and build the world where our many worlds will fit.

* * *

from Kristian E. Vasquez

What the Zapatistas teach me, and what the *compas* from *Esquadrón 421* are teaching Europe by listening and encountering networks, collectives, and organizations in resistance, is patience with each other—knowing that struggle will not achieve liberation tomorrow, but that our cultivation of another world grows from the earth when attended to. The mountain has come to Europe, and soon it will reach other places and other territories for life. We no longer have a world to win—as we are already part of another world surging from below—but we have a planet, *nuestre tierra madre*, to care for. We have a planet to tend to, a fire to re-awaken.

With these pieces, we walk while asking questions, we travel so we might listen, we encounter so might learn. We came to Spain not looking for answers, but to learn how Europe struggles from below against capitalism, patriarchy, colonial legacies, racism, borders, States, and other relations or forms of domination. From this reality and our own experiences, we came to understand ourselves as part of *medios libres*. In that spirit we share our *palabra* so others might listen, see, and witness too.

From *Slumil K'ajxemk'op*, or *Tierra Insumisa*.

Territorios en Resistencia.

Madrid, España.

Planeta Tierra.

—August 13, 2021

* * *

On the demonstrations in response to the CNI CIG and EZLN call to action, the following are descriptive reflections of the demonstration on August 13th, 2021 in Madrid following the call to decentralized action.

* * *

from Gustavo García

The day was August 13th and the time was 5:00 pm. It was broadcasted to be one of the hottest days in Madrid. The streets and skyscraper buildings were filled with messages of rebellion. We walked to our meeting place, in the heart of the downtown area. In the Plaza del Carmen, we gathered to reflect on our struggles, to acknowledge the possibilities, and to plant seeds of global resistance.

After two days of *mesas de trabajo*, we came together to prepare ourselves for what was to come. The organizers handed each one of us roses that became part of this exchange. We formed a circle and with a bandana; we created an altar right in the center. People introduced themselves, their struggles, and their vision for the future. Everyone shared their *palabra* and spoke about their struggles in geographies across Europe, Mexico, and the U.S. As the only delegates there from the U.S. and members of Sexta Grietas del Norte, we shared the struggles that inspired us, the ones that motivate us, the ones that fuel us to do the work of collective freedom. The altar, a collective creation, was the physical manifestation that acknowledged collective, local, international, and global struggle.

One by one, people shared their struggles. Slowly they cut up their flowers and placed pieces on the altar. An intimate moment. A time of humanization. A time of recognition. A time for recalibrations of previous conceptions. We opened a portal to see where we overlap, to see where Europe from below and to the left intersects with the below and the left from Mexico and the United States. And right when it was about to end, acts of kindness moved people in the space.

First, a *Mexicana* journalist Daliri was given a rose for their commitment to documenting movements. A writer for and of the people. Traveling and documenting manifestations of collectivity. The tears of love and compassion quickly changed the mood. It was followed by another act of kindness. This time from Manuel, a diasporic Mexican from Guerrero now living in France. He gave me a rose and recognized the struggles of Mexican-Indigenous-Chicanx migrants living in the United States and contesting colonialism. *Como dicen los Zapatistas, la Gira por la Vida es la colectivización de pueblos en el mundo que son de abajo y a la izquierda.*

Gracias compas.

Escribiendo desde las trincheras de tlayudas y rebeldía.

* * *

from Maritza Geronimo

Amidst the colonial landscape, thousands gathered for the anniversary of the fall of Tenochtitlán in 108 F degree heat. The *Esquadron 421* arrived at the *Plaza del Sol* and began to board a big yellow ship decorated with EZLN flags, balloons, and colorful banners. The ship sailed the streets of Madrid amongst an ocean of chants. *"Zapata vive! La lucha sigue y sigue"* (Zapata lives! The struggle continues and continues)! *"La tierra no se vende, se ama y se defiende"* (Land is not to be sold, it is to be loved and defended)!

The *compas* of *Esquadrón 421* traveled by ship to Spain and arrived at the port of Vigo on June 22, 2021. A Spanish *compa* shared that this port was where the first ship returning from the "new" world disembarked with foods, gold, and Indigenous peoples from the Americas. The Spanish ships brought violence and death to the Americas and returned to proudly show off the evidence of their "discoveries." Now the Zapatistas return to Spain on a ship not with the purpose of imposing a new world view but to instead build networks from below and to the left.

The yellow ship traveled the urban streets of Madrid, a symbolic image for all those watching to remember what happened not so long ago. Just 500 years later Indigenous *pueblos* enter *Centro Colon* and are once again face to face with Christopher Columbus.

* * *

from Natalia Toscano

Walking from Plaza del Carmen to the Plaza del Sol to participate in the Zapatista *manifestación*, the buildings reverberated with pulses of a familiar rhythmic drum. The *círculo de danza* Guerreros de La Luz offered a ceremony and prayer in honor of the 500 years of Indigenous resistance and life. Standing in the middle of the Plaza, the group assembled an altar and invoked the four directions and called towards the *antepasados*, the ancestors.

The *danza* visibly transformed the plaza, creating a spectacle for tourists who clearly did not understand what was happening. The unfamiliarity and curiosity written upon their faces, as they stood and uttered questions and commentary. Those from *España* (or at least perceived to be) also strolled by, took pictures, and watched as the *danzantes* transformed Madrid into another world, distinct from their everyday.

The *danzantes* in their act of bringing ceremony to the Plaza del Sol, opened a portal intended to celebrate the ancestors who lived and died in the struggle against colonialism. Their ceremony created spiritual ties with the people across the world who, in the now, continue the struggle for life and fight against the destructive systems and forces that aim to foreclose an Indigenous future. The ceremony, like the Zapatistas, marked this moment as the commencement of a new era. An era that will bring forward new possibilities for Indigenous peoples and all peoples in struggle.

The *danza* held in synergy with the *manifestación* provided a needed moment of reflection and shift in movement building. Forcing *La Otra Europa* to witness alternative acts of rebellion that look and feel different from marching and chanting. A reminder that there are other acts that propel us forward in our missions to build other worlds, other forms of being, and other forms of relating.

Tiahui.

* * *

from Kristian E. Vasquez

We arrived at *La Plaza de Colón*, or Columbus Plaza, close to 9 p.m. GMT in Madrid after marching for what felt like 500 years. Among the crowd marching, chanting, and singing for life and against Spain/Europe from above, you could see faces from all over the world. I marched alongside the anti-fascists, feminists, hooligans, punks, anarchists, Marxists, Black radicals, Mapuches, Xican@s, Spaniards, Mexicans, Latinxs, Arabs, Italians, Catalans, and a group waving a Palestinian flag among others in the crowd who became a voice that yelled, *No nos conquistaron*, they did not conquer us.

Many of us had prepared for this march as medios libres to accompany others who were engaged in autonomous documentation and media. As the compa Natalia called it, while we participated in an encounter at Esta es una plaza, we, Xicana Tiahui, were doing "insurgent documentary." Many of us found ourselves running and chasing pictures of banners, t-shirts, the Zapatistas on the big yellow boat, and moments that caught our eyes as we also sang with the people.

We followed the march as we arrived at the final destination that was full of symbolic monuments that marked the Zapatista encounter with Spain. Towering over us was a statue on a pillar of Italian-Genoese navigator Cristoforo Colombo (created in 1892), a giant bust sculpture named Julia (2018) by Jaume Plensa, and the Monumento al Descubrimiento de América (1970) that documents Spain's narration of its own encounter with Las Américas adjacent to the huge *Bandera de España*, the Spanish flag, that waved in the night.

In the face of these monuments to Spain's initiation into modernity, the *Esquadrón 421* disembarked their symbolic yellow boat to climb the steps of the monument to the supposed "discovery" of *Las Américas* to speak to Spain from below.

One of the Zapatista *compas* approached the mike to commence their announcement entitled "Only 500 Years Later," acknowledging the hospitality of the people from Spain and spoke their truth from their world:

We are Zapatistas of Mayan roots.

> We are from a geography called Mexico and we crossed the
> ocean to say these words to you, to be with you, to listen to you,
> to learn from you.
>
> We are from Mexico and in you and with you we find
> endearment, care, respect.

From their small corner of the world, Southeast Mexico, the Zapatista compas spoke of their struggles with recognition from the bad government of the Mexican state, but they were also there to share how 501 delegates of the Zapatistas, the National Indigenous Congress, the Indigenous Governing Council, and the Peoples' Front in Defense of the Land and Water, were traveling in parts to *Tierra Insumisa*. The struggle to travel to *La Otra Europa*, the Other Europe, was shared to all:

> All have suffered to get papers and vaccinations. They have
> gotten sick and have gotten well. They have felt hunger and have
> been away from their families, their communities, their land,
> their language, their culture.

The Zapatistas are not here in *Tierra Insumisa* to share their experiences, they are here to directly learn from the struggles of Europe, from the people themselves. In that process, they then play a part in weaving struggles, confronting differences, and in proposing that those who fight for life are struggling together. They continue:

> But we have learned that seeds are exchanged, sown, and grown
> on a daily basis, in our respective soil, with the knowledge of
> each person.
>
> Tomorrow is not born in the light. It is cultivated, cared for, and
> born in the unnoticed shadows of the early morning, when the
> night begins to cede terrain.

The seeds of rebellion, that is *Zapatismo*, traveled to Europe. They are not asking for us/them to adopt their ways, their geographies, nor their modes of organizing resistance. No. They ask us to move with the rage that sparks our spirit.

It is not about abandoning convictions and struggles. On the contrary. We think that the struggles of women, otroas, workers, natives, not only should not stop, but should be deeper and more radical. Each one faces one or more heads of the Hydra.

Because all those struggles, of yours and of us Zapatista Peoples, are for life.

But as long as we do not destroy the monster in its heart, those heads will continue sprouting and changing shape but with greater cruelty.

Their words for struggling from below and to the left acknowledge the struggle to embrace new tactics, new strategies, and changing forms of how we resist to fully destroy *La Hidra Capitalista*, the capitalist hydra. All struggles for life are valid in our movement in, against, and beyond capitalism as the form and relations of domination that the Zapatistas believe to be our general antagonism.

But, just as in every corner of the planet, in every beating heart, there is a misfortune present and another to come, there is also a resistance, a rebellion, a struggle for life.

Because living is not only not dying, it is not about surviving. Living as human beings is living with freedom. Living is art, it is science, it is joy, it is dance, it is struggle.

The struggle for life is a struggle for each and one of our hearts, beyond humanity, the heart of the Earth itself. As human peoples we fight for our existence on this Earth, to love and live.

Because we Zapatista communities have come to listen and learn the history that exists in each room, in each house, in each neighborhood, in each community, in each language, in each way and in each oh well.

With this rally at the end of the march, the Zapatistas shared their word. They showed that they were listening to the word from below, to sow and grow. They called on *Tierra Insumisa* to cultivate their own struggles for life, to weave and listen too. To show the world that they too are rebellion against domination.

Their word, which was published by Enlace Zapatista the early morning the next day, was signed as follows:

> On behalf of the Zapatista communities.
> The Zapatista Maritime Squadron, named "Squadron 421."
> Planet Earth. August 13, just 500 years later.

The crowds cheered loudly, "E-Z-L-N." We witnessed *Tierra Insumisa*, another Europe from below and to the left. We struggle with them.

From *Slumil K'ajxemk'op*, or *Tierra Insumisa*.

Territorios en Resistencia.

Madrid, España.

Planeta Tierra.

Compas and collectives from across Slumil K'ajxemk'op invited us to build an altar together in ceremony moments before the August 13, 2021 march on Madrid's Columbus Plaza

The *circulo de danza* Guerreros de la Luz

Top: Lola Sepúlveda of CEDOZ (Centro de Documentación Zapatista [Zapatista Documentation Center]) gives a talk on the history of the Zapatistas in the days before the August 13 march on Columbus Plaza

Bottom: Artists change a metro stop's name to "Bienvenidas Zapatistas" ("Welcome Zapatistas")

Opposite: Graffiti on a Madrid street: "Welcome EZLN"

Top: Squadron 421 boards a decorated boat on wheels for the march to Columbus Plaza

Bottom: March participants follow behind Squadron 421 to say "THEY DID NOT CONQUER US"

Opposite page: Squadron 421 reaching Columbus Plaza

The August 13, 2021 march culminated with Squadron 421 reading the communiqué "Only 500 Years Later" in front of the Monument to the Discovery of America

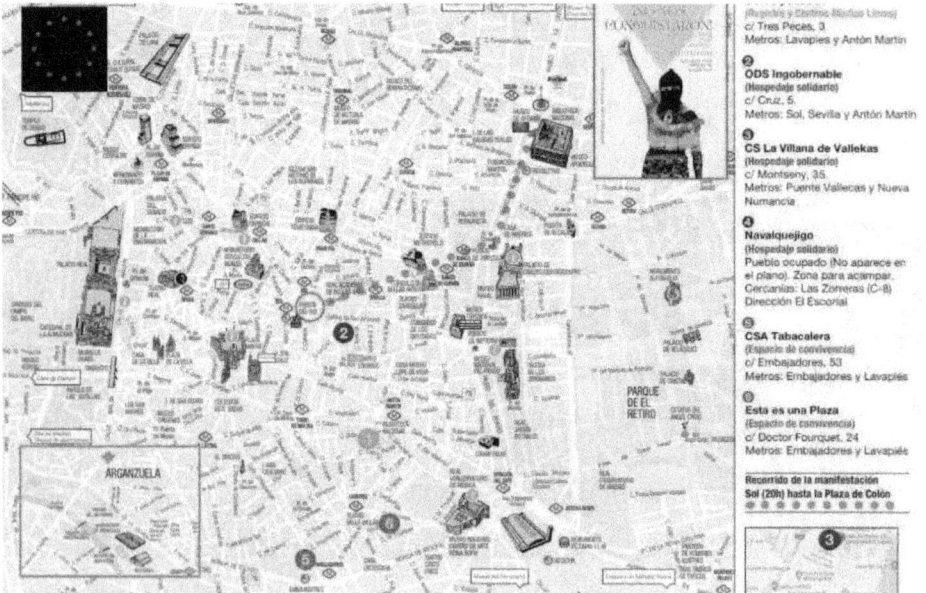

Map of the August 13, 2021 march from Puerta del Sol to Columbus Plaza

Top and bottom: The board game *Zapatista Autonomy: Collective Construction of the Autonomous Territory* was sold across Europe as a fundraiser for the Zapatistas' and CNI's tour. The game was "designed collaboratively by people and collectives in solidarity with the Journey for Life, 2021." To learn more, visit https://viajezapatista.eu/wp-content/uploads/Ingles.pdf

Ke Petiu Hein+, What Did You Dream Of?: Autonomy and Healing in Azqueltán

Sexta Grietas Health Brigade

In November 2021, members of Sexta Grietas del Norte joined a health brigade that traveled to San Lorenzo de Azqueltán, Mexico, to inaugurate the community's recently completed autonomous clinic. Azqueltán is a half-day's trip by car from Guadalajara, in the state of Jalisco, in the municipality of Villa Guerrero. Home to both the Tepehuano and Wixárika peoples, the community is cradled deep in the majestic Bolaños River Canyon. Surrounded by soaring cliffs, the remote territory is home to a wealth of natural riches, including the pitaya cactus, oaks, maguey, and a host of medicinal herbs and plants, as well as minerals. And all this makes the region coveted by profit-seekers who regularly threaten and physically attack the community using narco and paramilitary forces.

Establishing an autonomous health clinic is a fundamental part of the Tepehuano and Wixárika peoples' resistance strategy in Azqueltán. Autonomous institutions replace nonviable government institutions with community-based structures, and an autonomous clinic allows a measure of independence from a negligent, racist, and Western-science dominated institution of the "white robes." Creating their own healing institutions allows communities to develop and nurture practices from below that are grounded in a harmonious relationship to the natural world based on dignity, respect, appreciation, and mutual nourishment. The Zapatistas, who have taught the world these lessons by developing their own education, justice, and health systems, serve as a direct model and inspiration for Azqueltán.

Western, Socialist, and Indigenous medicine

Our connection to Azqueltán had been nurtured for years by a Grietas member whose family is from the community. As a ███████████, she was tasked with a *cargo*[1] to provide health services and facilitate the cooperative international effort. The Azqueltán Health Brigade she came to organize included ████████████████████, health professionals from India, nurses, herbalists, midwives, nutritionists, massage therapists, artists, and other practitioners. In order not to burden the community, two chefs from Grietas joined the group, organized the purchase of food, and worked with other *brigadistas* (Brigade members), and with women in the community to cook our meals. The kitchen hearth became an extension of the ceremonial fires, creating opportunities for being together, sharing, and bonding. And we found other ways to contribute by helping paint murals on the clinic's walls, translating for the health professionals, and caring for children so their mothers could receive treatment.

Azqueltán's autonomous clinic is based on a holistic, decolonized, from-below model of health and nutrition that draws from the best of both Western and Socialist medicine while centering the power of Indigenous medicine to ward off the destructive binaries of mind/body, collective/ individual, and material/ spiritual, often present in both. Thus, doctors on the Brigade could evaluate and treat their patients' medical issues while also assessing them for symptoms of trauma and anxiety, calling in other *brigadistas* to offer healing massage or ear acupuncture. A midwife led a women's circle and demonstrated the use of *rebozos* (shawls) as an aid to childbirth, while the community's women shared their plant remedies, as

---

1 A *cargo* (literally, a "load" or "burden") is a responsibility for a volunteer service that people in the community perform at the request of the community assembly.

well as their traumatic stories of having to give birth alone and of losing their children to untreated diseases. The Brigade's herbalists offered samples of plants they brought with them, and they, in turn, learned about the knowledges and practices of plant medicine from within the community.

Taking the path of autonomy, together

The Brigade had been invited to help inaugurate the clinic, to participate in traditional ceremonies celebrating its opening, and to commemorate the community's decision to take the path of autonomy. Eight years before, in November 2013, Azqueltán's assembly formally took up autonomy as a resistance strategy.[2] Its community assembly, a collective body composed of *comuneros*,[3] is the ultimate authority within Azqueltán's governance structure. Their communal decision-making is based on pre-colonial forms of government that are still practiced throughout Mexico in many Indigenous communities. In recent times, asserting autonomy has become an integral part of the struggle to protect Indigenous lands from dispossession and invasion driven by government efforts to impose capitalistic economic forms. It's a dispossession that often begins with the privatization of communally held land, forcing communities to defend themselves from violent takeovers by local *caciques*[4] who are supported by narco and paramilitary forces.

The village of Azqueltán is the political center of Tepehuano territory, originally comprising 230,000 acres stewarded for thousands of years before the Spanish Viceroy officially "granted" them the land in 1733. While the Viceroy introduced the alien colonizer notion of "ownership" of land, today those viceroyal acts are being strategically deployed by Indigenous peoples throughout Mexico as legal protection. Nevertheless, much of their territory continues to be taken over by invaders, including many

2 "Convocatoria al 5 aniversario del nombramiento de autoridades autónomas de Azqueltan" *Congreso Nacional Indígena*, https://www.congresonacionalindigena.org/2018/10/24/convocatoria-al-5-aniversario-del-nombramiento-de-autoridades-autonomas-de-azqueltan

3 *Comuneros* are members of the community, often heads of family, who work plots of land that are administered in common by the community.

4 A *cacique* is a person who exercises a lot of power in the political or administrative affairs of a town or region, using money or other influence to control the lives of the locals.

cattle ranchers, often facilitated by local governments under the control of wealthy invaders and "justified" by laws that allow people to take possession of communal indigenous lands that they claim are "vacant." The community is now in an intense struggle to prevent further dispossession from the remaining 93,000 acres to which they are legally entitled.

The Tepehuanos are joined in this struggle by the Indigenous Wixárika who originally arrived in Tepehuano territory fleeing Spanish settlers, and who continue to inhabit the remotest areas of the landscape. Resisting the state's efforts to assimilate them, the Wixárika have carefully preserved their language, their way of dress, and their spiritual traditions. They have also formed alliances with their Tepehuano brothers and sisters against Spanish invaders,[5] against the Mexican state, and more recently against incursions by capitalists seeking to profit off of resource extraction on their lands. In order to protect what remains of their land from invasions and from neoliberal government privatization schemes that allow the sale of common lands, and after decades of attempting to work through the official legal system, the Tepehuanos and Wixárika allied to take matters into their own hands and build autonomy together.

Guided by the Zapatistas and the National Indigenous Congress, their first step was to officially reinstate traditional forms of communal government, naming their own authorities in the assemblies, thereby forming a parallel Indigenous government that strategically deploys Mexican and international law to legally supersede the authority of local official government officials. The Wixárika and Tepehuana Autonomous Community of San Lorenzo de Azqueltán now participates in the National Indigenous Congress, a nation-wide network aligned with the Zapatistas and the principles of governance from below, collective work, defense of land and territory, and ceremony.

The importance of ceremony, rituals, and dreams

Ceremony is key to Azqueltán's autonomous project because it is how the community interprets knowledge of the land and communications from

5 https://en.wikipedia.org/wiki/Huichol

ancestors, providing guidance on how to recover the land together with their traditions, culture, language, and ways of healing. These practices continue in the face of violence: the local *caciques* who have benefited by invading Indigenous lands, have reacted with an extremely violent campaign against the most active *comuneros* who suffer multiple attacks, severe physical injuries, and deep trauma. Some *comuneros* no longer go to work in their lands for fear of being attacked, and other families have had to move out of the area temporarily.[6]

While the health brigade treated several of these community members for trauma, we learned that, despite the assaults, they remain firm in their commitment to recover and protect their lands, reflecting a spiritual conviction that is supported by healing ceremonies and spiritual traditions, including the interpretation of dreams that reveal the paths the community must take. This allowed us to better understand the Wixárika greeting *"Ke petiu hein+?"* (What did you dream of?") as an everyday reminder and practice of the guidance the community receives during ceremonies, rituals, and dreams. It was these practices that provided the community with the conviction that it was time to recuperate the land and propose a clinic that would provide "true health." The clinic and the Brigade were thus realizations of the community's collective dreams.

A key practice of autonomy in Indigenous territories, especially those belonging to the National Indigenous Congress, is the recovery of traditions and ceremonies that pertain to an ancestral cosmovision in which humanity is not the dominant species, as visualized by European tradition, but a part of nature, a being among other beings who must acknowledge and reciprocate the many gifts that nature provides for our sustenance. Ceremonial dances and offerings to Mother Earth at sacred sites are crucial to establishing such a harmonious, reciprocal relationship. The construction of autonomy thus connects the physical world with the spiritual; the territory that must be defended and protected is not just the physical land, but a place where the community constructs its collective life, both material and spiritual. "The clinic is meant to be a place of spiritual as well as physical healing," says Marcos, a Tepehuano

6 https://www.agendapropia.co/content/dual-isolation-displaced-indigenous-people-san-loren-zo-azquelt%C3%A1n

elected authority. Mario, a Wixárika trained in spiritual practices who was also elected as an authority, elaborates, "The body needs two kinds of medication, two types of curing; one having to do with [physical] discomforts and the other being the spiritual."

In ceremony, the community offers gratitude and sustenance to nature deities who then, in turn, send back energy and strength and offer guidance to the community. We were invited to participate in traditional ceremonies where offerings are made to Mother Earth, and energy and guidance is transmitted from the ancestors. Mario personally approached many of us, encouraging us to participate in the ceremonies and explaining how we could do so. He wanted us to learn about how to offer gratitude and sustenance to Mother Earth in order to receive her energy and strength. He said, "Mother Earth is hungry and thirsty just like we are. So we can all begin to live like this, to make offerings, to give to her, because the earth gives to us what we need and Mother Earth needs us to give to her, too." He wanted us to participate in the practices that Indigenous traditions offer "because making offerings to Mother Earth means giving her energy so that the same energy can strengthen humans. As Indigenous, if we don't do this, the struggle is worthwhile, but it proceeds very slowly. But when we walk with nature, we get much more strength, it gives us knowledge that we human beings cannot imagine [on our own]."

At the invitation of our hosts, we joined the community in a collective hike up to a sacred mountain site where we held candles as the Tepehuano dancers, dressed in their traditional garments, re-enacted their ancient stories. Later that evening, we moved to the town square and gathered around a roaring fire where the Wixárikas performed their dances. We were invited to share a drink of *rosita*[7] prepared with great love and care by our hosts. As we sat together by the fire until dawn, everyone was invited to share their thoughts. Some people spoke of their suffering from the violence of their adversaries, others spoke of the joy they felt at this gathering. Brigade members shared their awe and appreciation of our new brothers and sisters of the Azqueltán community. Many shared intimate feelings. We listened to the words of the *maracáme* (shaman),

7 *Rosita*, or *tutu*, is the name the Wixárika use to refer to "peyote," a term they do not like.

who counseled on practices of grieving and healing. As we gazed into the ceremonial fire, we felt it enter our bodies, creating an emotional and spiritual warmth that opened our hearts and bonded us to this project that, from that moment, expanded beyond the community of Azqueltán and into each one of our own geographies.

Dreaming collectively across geographies

After the ceremonies, there were more workshops, trainings, and health consultations. *Promotores de salud* (health promoters), members of the community who had been elected to learn and administer healing in the clinic, received training in basic practices such as drawing blood, taking blood pressure, administering shots and basic medicines. One glance inside the small clinic revealed how worlds apart it was from the Western medical system, where doctors seldom listen for more than a few minutes to patients before prescribing their remedies. Here the doctors listened carefully, asking questions about the patients' lives and wellbeing. They listened for and treated signs of emotional trauma, which many have suffered from the constant threat of violence. People from the surrounding community who had been refusing to participate in the construction of autonomy came by to be treated, or simply to witness the outpouring of care and camaraderie. We were later told that the autonomous authorities felt this was an important positive development for the communities. They noted that there was a lightness of spirit during those days of our gathering that had not been felt in the community for a long time, due to the darkness and dread cast by violence and harassment.

Many follow-ups are now being planned for this experience that moved us all so deeply—guests and community members alike.[8] In our report-back to the broader Sexta Grietas del Norte assembly, the Brigade was unified in expressing how much we had learned from the experience, including new understandings of our own processes of decolonization. Guests in a breathtakingly beautiful landscape, we were fortified by participating in this

8 *Brigadistas* continue the work of organizing virtual follow ups with patients and discussing continued training in health promotion and midwifery, supporting the recovery of ancestral childbirth traditions, cataloging and disseminating the community's endemic medicinal plants, and supporting in organizing women's circles and men's circles to address gender inequalities.

brave, collective struggle, and we were overwhelmed by the warmth and generosity of our hosts. The solidarity, the mutual respect, admiration, and love that comes with a shared vision of a world that could be, and that we are all committed to living for, will continue to inspire and energize us here in our resistances in *el Norte*, the other United States.

Azqueltan's children in front of the new clinic, "Hope and Life." Photo by Semillas.

Health promoters inaugurating the autonomous clinic. Photo by Semillas.

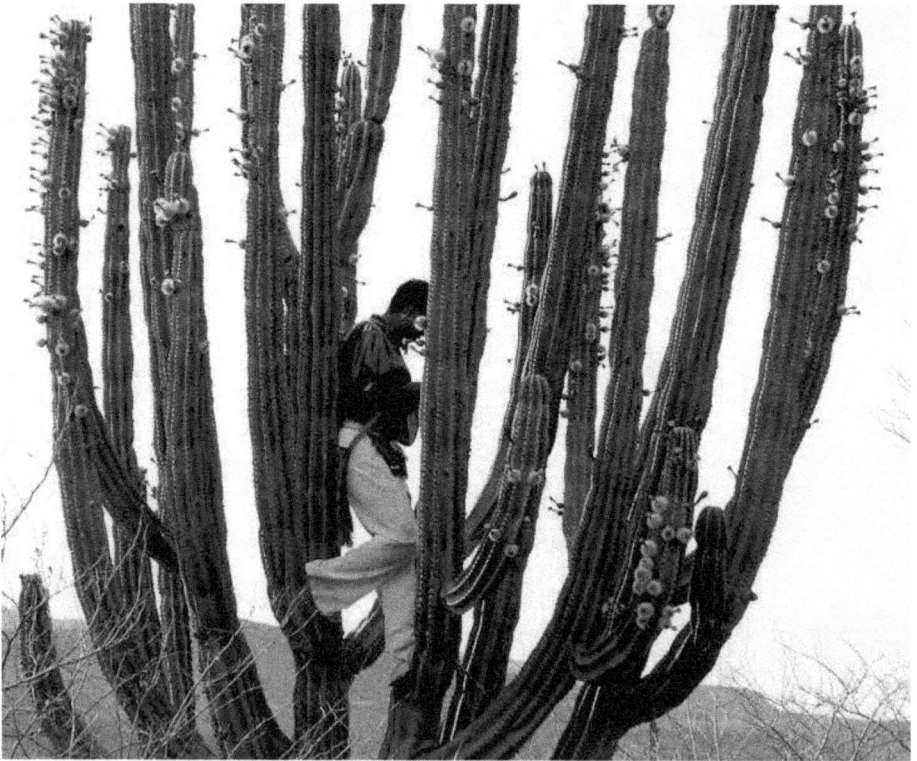

Top: The cliffs at the entrance to Bolaños Canyon. Photo by Caitlin Manning.

Bottom: Harvesting pitaya flowers. Photo by Hanna Wallis.

Opposite: The flowers of the sacred "tutu" offered during the traditional ceremonies. Photo by Semillas.

Top, bottom, and opposite: Ceremonies celebrating the opening of the clinic in Azqueltan.
Photos by Hanna Wallis.

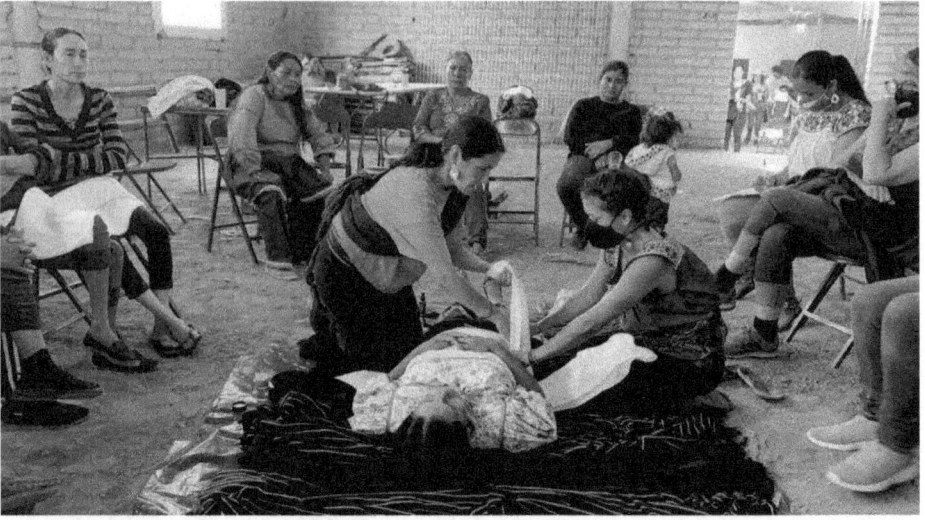

Top: Midwives from the health brigade offering workshops in *rebozo* techniques. Photo by Alé.

Opposite: Community members practicing tourniquet techniques. Photo by Caitlin Manning.

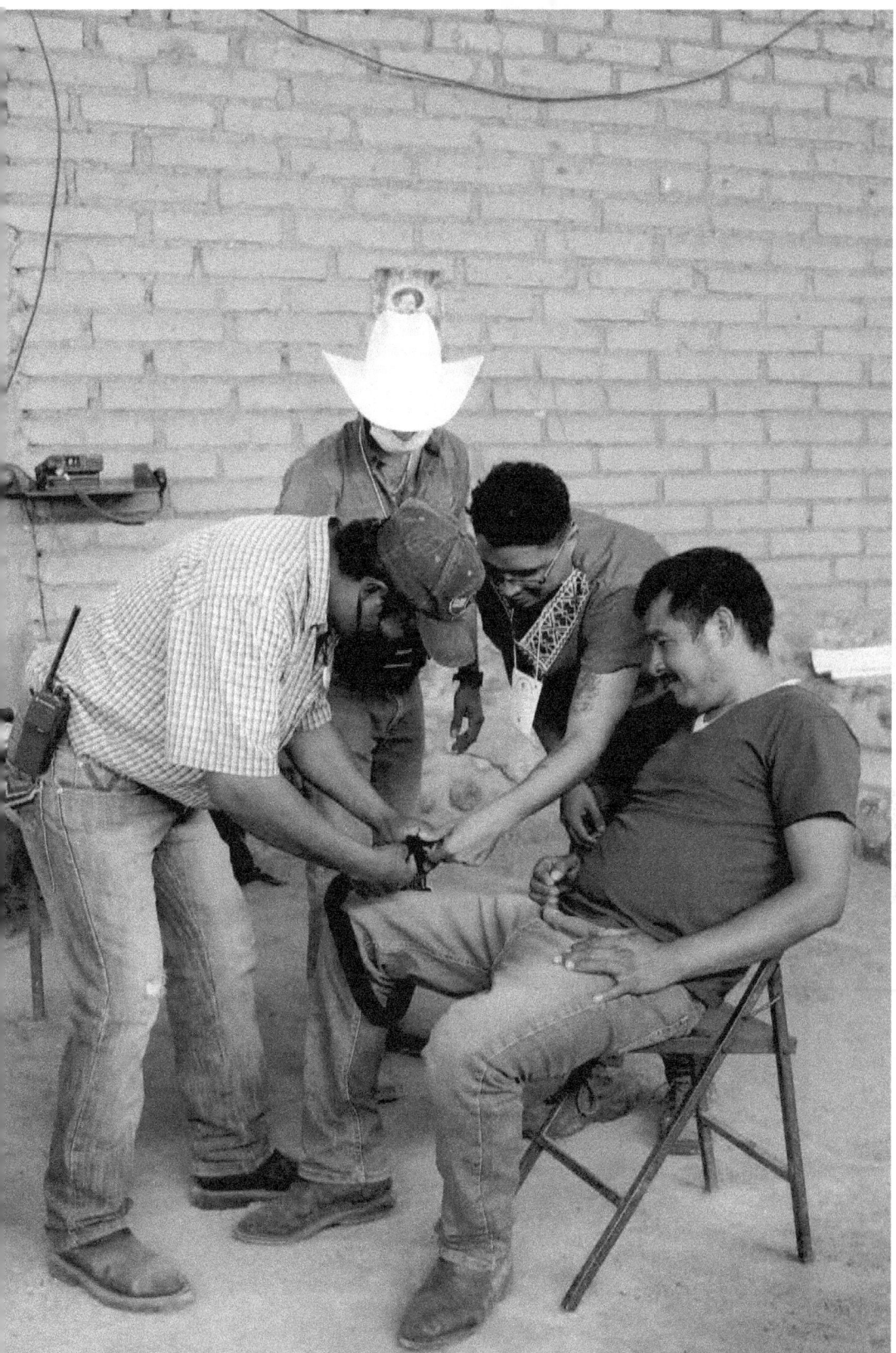

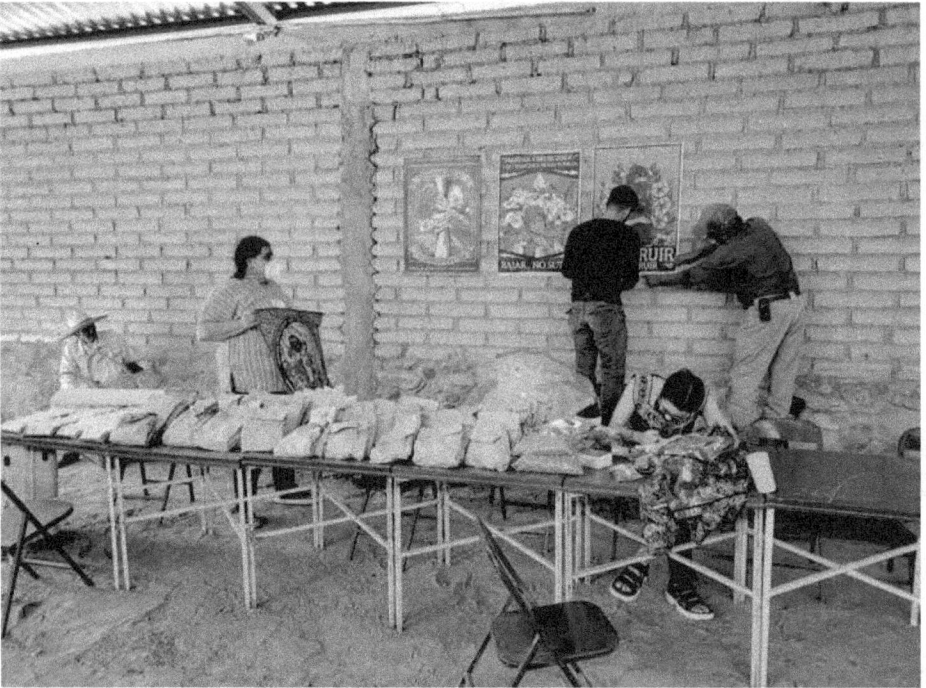

Opposite top: Herbalists from the health brigade offering herb samples while pinning up artwork of the 7 principles of leading by obeying. Photo by Pete Hesher.

Top and opposite: Azqueltan's church at the center of town. The ceremonies continue around the fire until dawn. Photos by Semillas.

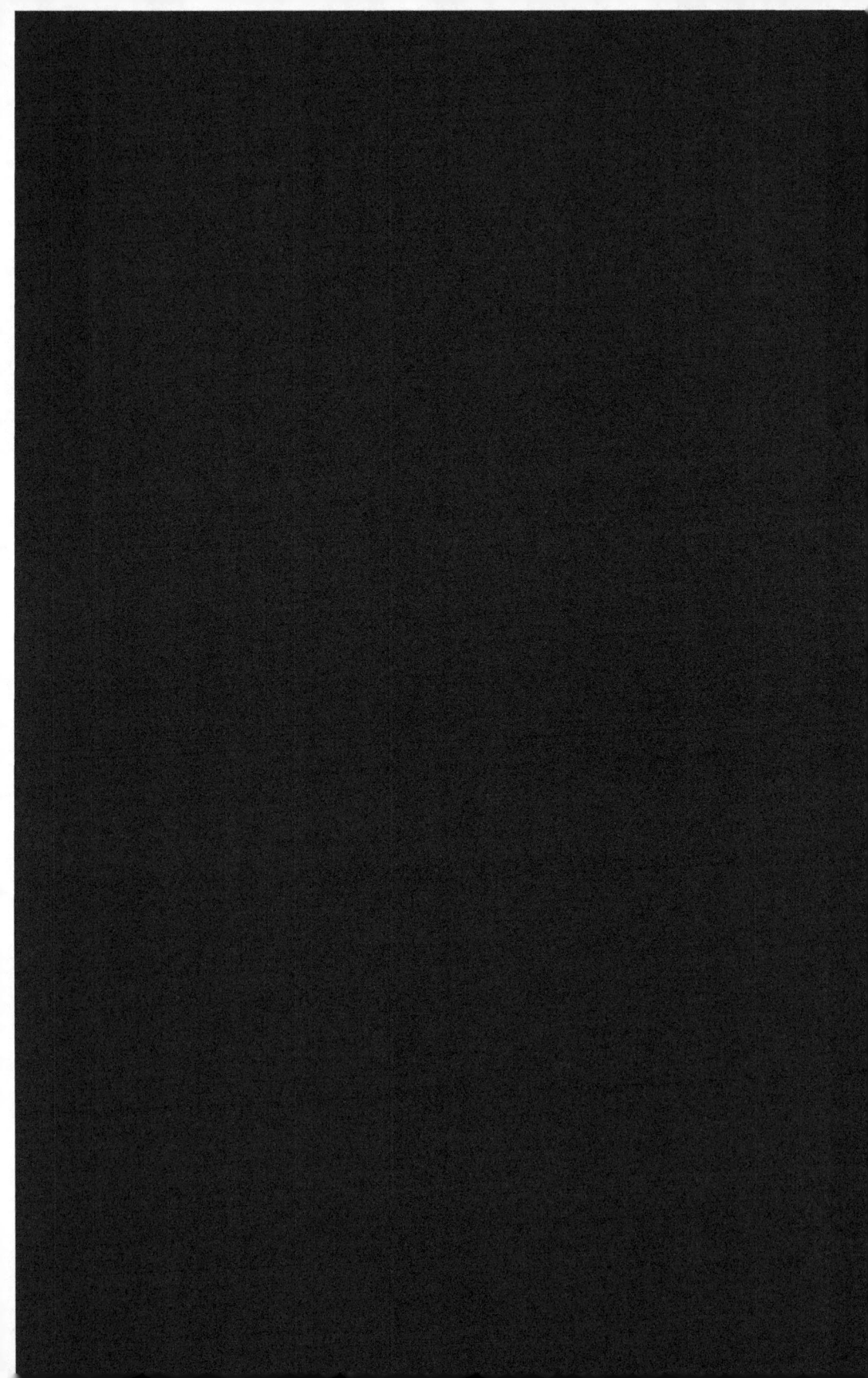

The Zapatista Women's Movement: An Interview with Rosaluz Perez

This interview, conducted by Nancy Serrano, is a transcript of the translation produced as Episode 2 of the "Zapatistas Podcast: Lessons and Stories from Chiapas" (August 23, 2021), an audio series that delves into the Zapatista movement from the early days of the "uprising to the present." Produced by the Galway Feminist Collective (Ireland) and Promedios Mexico. The original podcast is available at https://rss.com/podcasts/thezapatistaspodcast/255385

Rosaluz, I wanted to start by asking you how you got involved in Indigenous women's struggles, and what your first impressions were of the Zapatista movement.

I first got involved in the struggle of the Zapatista movement in 1995 when the government revealed the identity of Subcomandante Marcos.[1] It was a very important moment because the war and an offensive against the Zapatista communities was once again triggered. So an important solidarity campaign took place nationally. People started organizing spontaneously from many corners of Mexico and solidarity caravans were organized. It was at this time that I arrived in Chiapas.

Suddenly, when we arrived in a Zapatista community, a barrier of Zapatista women came out and told us we couldn't go through. It was a very strong image, for us coming from the city, of those women that we had always seen as being oppressed. At this moment, these women with all their strength were telling us that we could not pass into their community. And

---

1 Note from the editors: The Zapatistas have never confirmed the identity of the late Subcomandante Marcos.

they were alone. There were no men in the community at the time. That first impression really left a mark on me—that image, that first image of strength, organization and dignity.

I think it was something that marked all of us who came in that caravan, and it made me curious to want to understand what their struggle was about and why were those particular women involved? Who were they? I didn't know what I could learn from these women, but from that moment on, like many others in civil society, we got involved in the work in communities. Within a context of war, where everything was in a state of emergency, the Zapatista communities opened their doors to civil society to participate in the areas of education,health and human rights. That's how many people from civil society came to the communities and got involved in the everyday construction work within the villages. And I think it was a unique and very beautiful experience, those early years.

How interesting. So your first meeting was, as you said, directly with the women, and because I imagine the men were away at the time. Were they involved in the conflict perhaps?

At that moment, the men were in the cornfield or doing other work on their farms. It was the women who stayed home in the community, and I think this also gives us an image of the women as the guardians of the community.

Could you give us some historical background from what you know, around Zapatista women and their movement? What was their life like before the 1994 uprising?

So after this solidarity caravan arrived, we stayed in the community, and I asked what I could do to support their struggle. They told me that if I wanted to help with anything, I could train young people as community teachers. So that was my job over the next five years. And from this work I witnessed much of the everyday life of the people. And perhaps, I now understand a little about their history and women's aspirations.

I think it's very important to understand that the Zapatistas are Mayan peoples, and their communities come from a long history of struggle for the land. The organized Zapatista communities come from a first emancipation that took place in the 1970's when there was a massive struggle for land.

Most of the original Indigenous communities, they worked as indentured servants in Chiapas, which meant that they were workers in a plantation under conditions of semi-exploitation, both men and women: men in the fields and women worked in the landowners' houses, or were left in their own communities. That gave rise to the plantation system. A division of labor by gender: men in the fields, immigration outside the community, and women in charge of the community, in charge of raising children and everything that is necessary for life to be possible. And in addition, women worked doing domestic labor and childcare for the landowner. And all of this produces an entire cultural framework and an important division of labor that the Zapatistas have been dismantling over many years of struggle, and this is not so easy to do.

We are talking about women living in a system of a division of labor where domestic work, child care, and community survival falls mainly on their shoulders. And that's a job that starts at 3 a.m. and ends at 10 p.m. At night. They are the first to get up and the last ones to fall asleep. And that makes an important difference to their physical health, in addition to the fact that they have to stay at home in the community all the time. This also led to the fact

I think it's very important to understand that the Zapatistas are Mayan peoples, and their communities come from a long history of struggle for the land.

The Zapatistas rise up with two symbolic banners: one represents the land and the other the Women's Revolutionary Law.

that it is men who leave the community, and it's the men who are normally bilingual, while the women are monolingual.

In this period, it is the men who have access to a circle of contacts, be it in the city or with government projects. This allows the men to be recognized by local government as the heads or representatives of the communal lands. It positioned men as the decision-makers, from which women have been historically excluded in Indigenous communities, and that usually also led to women not being part of the Indigenous assembly, where decisions are made. So we're talking about a very complicated historical context that has placed men in decision-making spaces and leaves women responsible for the children and the community in general.

And I think it's very important to understand this in order to appreciate all that the Zapatistas have had to do. The trajectory they have had to do follow in order to break these internal and external bonds of oppression because it is something that the community has deeply internalized, but it also comes from the outside.

So, with that insight, into the heavy load on the complexities of the lives of Indigenous women in 500 years of colonialism. Can you tell us how they went about creating the Women's Revolutionary Law in the Zapatista movement that became public in 1994?

When the Zapatista uprising takes place, the Zapatistas rise up with two symbolic banners: one represents the land and the other one is the Women's Revolutionary Law. There were other laws, but those two are the most important.

When I say that it is very important to understand the context it is because this Woman's Revolutionary Law is declared by the Zapatistas so that more women can participate in the struggle, to open up more spaces for them to participate, for those Indigenous women to have the necessary autonomy to make decisions about their political participation and decisions on how to live their lives. But I think something that seems even more important to me than this Law is the process prior to this Revolutionary Law. That process has more to do with the originals of the actual organization. The EZLN, or the Zapatista army, has repeatedly said that there was a revolution within the revolution. The origins of that revolution have to do with the first women who became involved in the Zapatista struggle. These first women had no choice but to participate as military women in the EZLN military organization. They crossed new terrain so that today other women can participate differently within the Zapatista organization. And I think these first women involved in the struggle broke the mold. They overcame many obstacles within their communities and within their families as has been documented in many interviews with the first women soldiers. They had to overcome many obstacles within their families, the community, and within the organization in order to be in a position where they were listened to.

So, the fact that in 1993 the women managed to get their organization to draft a law, however simple it was, the Women's Revolutionary Law, is the result of all this effort that those first women had to make by breaking these old patterns. Not only this but also in the work they engaged, in working with the same communities and inviting them to participate in the organization. This work done by these women led to the creation of the first women's meetings where women had to question their history, their gender status for the first time, and be able to understand why their gender status was politically motivated.

Then these first women get involved in a war, which is a bizarre role

For a woman to agree to be part of a war implies that she is accepting that her children be involved in a war, that everything she has protected for centuries, being the guardians of the community, being responsible for the life in the community, is put at stake.

for an Indigenous woman. For a woman to agree to be part of a war implies that she is accepting that her children be involved in a war, that everything she has protected for centuries, being the guardians of the community, being responsible for the life in the community, is put at stake. So that's what I mean by a bizarre role for an Indigenous woman. Getting involved in a military struggle. For these women to have agreed to engage in a military structure before 1994 means a whole lot of work that could have been done only between women and between women who understand their own gender status. That's the background of the Women's Revolutionary Law. It is the public face of the work prior to 1994, which started in the 1980s.

NS: That's true. And it also shows us the seriousness of the situation in which they had to make a tough decision after a lengthy and deep process. Can you comment a little on the role that women have played in the recovery of territory and in creating autonomous lands?

As I mentioned already, the Zapatistas rise up with two principal banners: the land belongs to those who work it and Indigenous women's rights. I would say that they are the two major pillars in the Zapatistas' struggle. They haven't put it quite like this, but that's what we are learning from the past that followed. I think the two things are closely linked, because in the end the land makes life possible. They are people that came from a trajectory of struggle for the land, but life is possible because we can be a community, and we can be a community because we have the land at the center of life.

That is, even with the autonomy and the resistance that the Zapatistas have built, none of it would be possible if it weren't for Indigenous farming communities that produce their own food. And that's what allows them to really be a community, that's what allows them to build autonomy, that's what allows women to continue to enjoy a viable life in the community. All this is possible because a territory exists.

I also think that, for some of the women who provided testimonies I collected, the recovery of the land was very important because, first of all, this allowed them to free themselves from working for the landowners. But in addition, this meant that men did not have to migrate. Men can stay in the community and enjoy a life within that community. It also begins to change the gender division of labor, because if men are present in the community, they can hold government positions within their community, like positions within Zapatista autonomous structures. These positions now exist because they have land, land they can live off of. This was unthinkable for many communities before the uprising, when the communities were like dormitories, where men had to go work elsewhere, or work on the land of the wealthy owner to get their own food.

So since the seventies, the project of the division of labor by gender and the role of women and men in the community has been changing little by little. Could you tell us a little bit about how this has been carried out in practice since the uprising?

I think it's been a process. Perhaps this process has to do with the progress and women's participation in political positions, in roles in the autonomous communities, in military positions. That is, we are talking about communities in which women did not originally participate in the assemblies and a first step to being in the Zapatista organization is to include women in the local assemblies. This was a first step towards greater participation of women in decision-making. Then came participation in the pre-war military positions. After the war, came women's participation and civil autonomy positions, everything that has to do with autonomy. Then with the Zapatista Good Government Councils came women's participation in those committees and government structures and political structures. It happened little by little at the start. At first there was a small percentage of women and I think it was more or less from the good governance committees in their second year of existence that a law was passed that there be parity in political authorities. So we are already talking about another level of participation in policy and decision-making structures. I think that all this has been a very important benchmark, especially for young Zapatista women. Young Zapatista women no longer have had to fight to open up these spaces for participation. That is, those spaces are already open to them.

And this is creating a new generation of women. Very different from the women of 25 or 26 years ago, like the first women in the movement 30 years ago. So, I think this is constantly transforming and changing everyday life as well, because in order for a woman to take part in local government committees, she has to delay the age of marriage. As women have access to more information, they have access to being women in a different way within their community. In other words, there is no longer a single profile of a woman, which before was that of a mother and the caregiver of the home and community; now there is a range of possibilities of being a woman within the same community.

A woman can be a health promoter, she can have a political post, she can be a video promoter or a teacher. All this provides a range of possibilities that also revolutionizes the thinking of younger women. It has been very important in that transformation of women's daily lives.

This has also created an awareness of different ways of living, of being a woman. But I also think that the whole Zapatista process has been a process of realizing that there are different forms of relations. Before, communities had the relationship with the government and with the church, and now they have a relationship with the wider world with different ways of thinking, different ways of being.

So that means nowadays women can decide who they marry. Is this how it is in other Indigenous communities?

The first point in the Women's Law says that women can decide who to marry, and that law becomes less necessary each time because it is increasingly a concrete reality in each community. And not only can Zapatista women decide who they marry, but *whether* they want to marry or not, whether they want to be single mothers or get married or get divorced. That was something very interesting from the first cases that the Good Government Councils resolved in the area where I worked. I saw many non-Zapatista couples that came to solve their problems with the Zapatistas, because the young people wanted to get divorced, but in their community they were not allowed. They thought that if they went to the Zapatista authorities with the Good Government Councils, they would be backed up and be able to divorce. That's very interesting to me as the Zapatistas also became references for non-Zapatista communities, for young people from non-Zapatista communities.

Well, in the urban world in which most of us from the Western world live in, women are accustomed to a style of feminism with more emphasis on individual rights. You've already told us a bit about what Indigenous women's lives are like, that they are a very important

There is no longer a single profile of a woman, which before was that of a mother and the caregiver of the home and community; now there is a range of possibilities of being a woman within the same community.

nucleus for the community in food production. And what would you see as the main differences between Western feminism and thus Zapatista women's movement?

I would say that one of the main differences between the individual versus the collective is that for a long time, Western feminism fought for equal rights between men and women, but often it was a certain type of feminism, focused more on women as individuals. I think that for Zapatista women, this long journey they have undertaken and all the changes they have achieved, is rooted in an initial collective aspiration. In many of the testimonies gathered in the first interviews, they say that they were involved in the Zapatista struggle to change the conditions of their family, of their communities, and also to change their own conditions. In other words, this brought about change for them as well. It was also an opportunity for them to escape their horizon, their destiny as women, which they didn't want. As women, they were not allowed to escape their set destinies before the uprising. But they also said that by taking this step of trying to change this destiny, they were taking a step for other women.

I think the motivation behind Zapatista women always comes from their collective aspiration, the whole construction of autonomy. The Zapatistas themselves have a structure where individuation stems from the collective work. As women grow up,

Western feminism fought for equal rights between men and women, but often it was a certain type of feminism, focused more on women as individuals.

they are empowered. They have a voice for participating in the construction of the collective, and you can see this with the newer generations. You now see a 15-year-old girl talking to an auditorium of 2,000 people with such strength! And the historical burden they carry. The individual is not put first to then achieve some impact for the community, but the communal pushes the individual to grow and do better. I think this has been one of the most valuable lessons I have learned from the trajectory of those women.

Could you talk to us a bit about the women's collective work?

Much of the work of these women's groups began in the years prior to the uprising, from groups organized by the Diocese. These specific women's spaces were very important because they were the first spaces that created an opening that meant women could travel from one community to another. Women in the communities knew how to take advantage of the Diocese and the networks to work with women to meet their own goals and shape their own interests, later on for more political interests, and also allowed them to become involved in Zapatismo.

We could say that women's collectives played a part in the history of community organizing. And throughout the construction of autonomy, women have also created several spaces only for women to address their needs

> I think the motivation behind Zapatista women always comes from their collective aspiration, the whole construction of autonomy.

around raising children around their specific need as health promoters and so on. Not only have they been collective work spaces, they've also been women's assemblies where solely women's issues are addressed.

In the area of health, there has also been a lot of work on reproductive rights. There are clinics, for example, in La Garrucha, that are especially for women. I think this also permeates into the vision of Zapatista autonomy. We are talking about the liberation of women brought about by women who have had a heavy historical burden, who have seven or eight children. We're talking about women who are viewed as a oppressed by Western feminism. It is these oppressed women who have taken steps towards building the liberation of younger women. And I think it's a very important message. From my perspective I see all these women as the protagonists of a very complex system of community transformation. It's those protagonists who, from a Western feminist perspective can be seen as oppressed women. So it's a very a very important difference. It's like a paradox: it is these women who are apparently oppressed who are building a path to liberation.

I just want to explain a little to our listeners because some of these women's collectives that are part of the San Cristobal Diocese of the Catholic Church in Chiapas are part of a group called CODIMUJ which is short for in La Coordinadora Diocesana de Mujeres (Diocese

> It is these women who are apparently oppressed who are building a path to liberation.

Coordination of Women). This is the only exclusive women's area in the whole of the Catholic Church. So could you tell us about the CODIMUJ and the role that it has played in women's organizing in Chiapas?

When I talk about these collectives in the Diocese, it is something historical. This all begins before the uprising. I think that each region was organized in different ways, but a very important role in some regions were groups of women that were formed by pastoral workers, by nuns who also fought within the Catholic Church itself, and within the Diocese of San Cristobal.

In other words, they also opened a door to work exclusively with women because of the empathy they generated with women in communities. They also had to fight within the Diocese of San Cristobal to be allowed to run these groups of women. That seems very important to me. And these women's groups, once they're created in communities, when a community starts organizing, you can sow the seed. But you no longer know what will happen to that seed. So I believe that all this work done by the Church, all this work centered on their having access to communication and making collectives allows them to organize themselves to get involved from below and later to organize their own autonomy, not with Church groups but with their own groups from the autonomous process.

I think it is very valuable work. But that work originally carried out by these pastoral workers of peace from the Diocese, the Zapatista women collected these seeds and then formed their own collectives within their autonomous structure. That's what happened to us with everything. We worked a little on education, and the Zapatistas arrived and grabbed it with their hands and modified it to their needs.

Yes, that's a very interesting story, and it's very unique as well. I know you have told us some of the lessons and your learnings with the Zapatistas, and that's one of the focuses of this podcast series to point out what we can all take away from the Zapatista experience and apply it to our lives, our struggles. So what lessons most stand out to you, what do you think are the main lessons?

What can we can learn from the Zapatista women's movement? For women in Ireland or anywhere in the world?

I think that, for me, the most important lesson to understand, and that we need to reflect on from the Zapatista teachings, is first, how do you make yourself into a better human based on the construction of the collective? That's something very important to me. And I think that's how they were built. They had a concern, and then took steps towards collective construction. They have grown and opened the way for new generations of women.

I would say a second lesson is learning by doing. Every step taken by the Zapatistas has been a practical step for the next step. Every gathering or event they have organized has been an exercise for the next one. All the time they practicing and all the time they are doing. It takes a collective way above all, rather than a lot of resources. It's not that resources aren't important, but I think at the heart of its construction, for me, is the collective will and how to realize it, how to learn and do together. For me, I think these are the two most important lessons.

Apparently, you can build something out of nothing. I feel like they don't have any obstacles, like you can build out of thin air. If you have this collective will and if you're sure about what your dreams are and what you want to pursue. For me, these are the three most important lessons.

I think that, for me, the most important lesson to understand, and that we need to reflect on from the Zapatista teachings is, first, how do you make yourself into a better human based on the construction of the collective?

Well, thanks to Rosaluz for such a thought-provoking and personal insight into the Zapatista women's movement, learning about how these strong Indigenous women have overcome so many obstacles and continue to do. So, it is very inspirational: bettering ourselves to build collectives, learning by doing, not being afraid of making mistakes, and constructing our collective dreams. Now, I feel that's what the Zapatista women are inviting us to do with their European tour. And to shake us awake, and get to it. Are you up for it?

Building *Corazón Nosótrico*: A Zapatista Seed Pedagogics[1]

Charlotte M. Sáenz

There exists a decolonizing education process seeded by the Zapatista movement that extends its reach far beyond its autonomous territories. I call this process a "Zapatista Seed Pedagogics." This naming is a way to understand the political-educational and ethical framework rooted in traditional ancestral Indigenous ways of knowing and being in relationship to other (human and non-human) beings. This pedagogics draws on the seed, with both its material and symbolic roles in our survival and vital evolutionary potential. This theoretical intervention acknowledges the Zapatista movement's historical roots in Marxism, liberation theology, Mayan cosmologies, and pedagogies of the oppressed. Seed pedagogics transcend nation-state and identity borders while remaining grounded in ancestral ways of knowing, being, and doing embodied in the languages and practices of Indigenous peoples. Zapatista Seed Pedagogics develops from what is known as Zapatismo, today known throughout the world as an emancipatory, educational, and political-ethical movement rooted in ancestral knowledge and political practices interrelated with the web of life.

1 Translated from the original Spanish of a modified excerpt from Sáenz et al. (2021)

Zapatismo is part of a centuries-long hemispheric history of Indigenous resistance and rebellion against the ongoing colonial-capitalist oppression experienced continentally across Abya Yala[2] and across the globe. It evolves in solidarity with other oppressed peoples grappling with similar historical conditions of domination. Together, they confront a globally homogenizing, cisheteropatriarchal, racialized capitalism[3]—one whose intensified accumulation-extraction since 1492 has greatly accelerated in the last half-century, heightening numerous existing crises while causing mass extinction of habitats and species on the planet. A Zapatista Seed Pedagogics draws on both the material and symbolic roles of the seed to reveal the potency and potential of life itself; it creates an "intergalactic" learning space for political imagination, inspiration, and exchange among those seeking more liberatory ways of living, as Zapatismo constantly reformulates itself both within its own struggle, as well as in conversation and exchange with other social movements.

A Zapatista Seed Pedagogics enacts a consciousness-raising process among those who rebel and resist. Throughout the greater part of three decades, Zapatismo has been in dialogue with numerous intellectuals, activists, peasants, artists, scientists, and other social movements around the world who are also in process of defending their land, bodies, territories, and planetary life. Exchanges among these diverse peoples have created an extensive educational process that goes beyond any particular social movement's pedagogy. Thus, Zapatismo enacts what Dussel (2019) describes as a "Pedagogics of Liberation," bringing together philosophical, ethical, political, and economic meanings.

What is pedagogics?

Enrique Dussel distinguishes between pedagogy, the science or technique of transmitting knowledge (that assumes a universal, liberal,

2 Abya Yala is the name given to the American continent by the Kuna people, meaning "land of vital blood or potency."

3 In examining global nation-state economic relations, a world-system theory attributed to the American sociologist Immanuel Wallerstein (1974) describes the global dominance of a capitalist economy enriched by the ongoing colonization of peripheral and semi-peripheral economies.

equality), and pedagogics,[4] a part of philosophy that—together with ethics, politics, and economics—considers face-to-face relationships in contexts of inequity (2019). Rotating governance by all members of the community is only one way the Zapatistas enact this kind of pedagogics. First and foremost, a liberatory pedagogics requires listening to the voice of alterity:

> In pedagogics the Other's voice signifies content revealing itself, and liberatory education can only begin with the revelation of the Other. [...] Mutual listening is an essential part of a praxis that allows a relationship to grow within a politics ethics of equality.

Dussel affirms that this "pedagogics of liberation" is exercised by procreative subjects who contribute to the educational process, encouraging mutual learning through the method of liberatory critique. Importantly, the method should not impose, but rather champion a collaborative, inter-subjective creativity as the engine of liberatory action.

Drawing from this reading of Dussel's *Pedagogics of Liberation*, while considering its other influences (Mayan cosmologies, Paulo Friere's *Pedagogy of the Oppressed*, Samuel Ruíz's[5] "Indian theology," and Marxist currents), I theorize a Zapatista Seed Pedagogics as a self-reflexive, unlearning and co-teaching process that builds awareness and action in defense of life itself. Zapatista Seed Pedagogics unfolds both inside and outside of Zapatista autonomous communities, and across various geographies, evidenced by their current *Travesía Por la Vida*, their Journey for Life, across the five continents announced and launched in 2021 with Europe as its first destination. It is from these fertile encounters between the Zapatistas and peoples outside their autonomous territories, that a collective political subject emerges.

4 In translating from the Spanish "pedagógica" into the English "pedagogics," Backer and Diego (2019) create an ambiguity as to its singular/plural use, one fittingly appropriate as it confers a flexibility to refer to a specific pedagogics, while also allowing for there to be others.

5 Samuel Ruiz García, a Mexican Catholic priest and defender of the rights of Indigenous peoples. He was bishop in Chiapas from 1959 to 1999 where he promoted liberation theology. He was a mediating figure between the government and the EZLN during the 1994 San Andrés dialogues. He learned several local Indigenous languages and is called "tatik" by the Indigenous people of Chiapas, which means "father."

Integrating relationship

A Zapatista Seed Pedagogics seeks to re-integrate false separations and simple dualities (such as body/mind, male/female, self/other) imposed by the colonial-capitalist mentality that emerged as part of the project of modernization. Zapatismo builds on an already existing Indigenous *comunalidad*[6] (Maldonado 2003), a relationship of being "in common" with all other beings: plants, animals, mountains, rivers, forests, spirits, the cosmos, and even the dead. Wherever these Indigenous collective practices still hold, these relationships manifest in a common immanence of daily life. They are present in the many rituals of collectivity that accompany healing, learning, governance, celebration, and agriculture across Abya Yala. A Zapatista Seed Pedagogics politicizes these practices while also re-integrating the Modern separation between heart/head or mind/body. As a *sentipensante*[7] (thinking-feeling) approach to the world and existence (Barbosa 2015), the heart serves as an important location for knowing. Thinking with one's heart, and not just one's head as is conventionally privileged from a Eurocentric perspective, is a way to access felt connections arising from the body's multiple senses as well as trusting the intuition of all these when considered holistically and collectively. This larger sourcing of knowledge builds an ethical and political *corazón nosótrico*, a collective heart, (*o'tan* in Tseltal;[8] *yo'on* in Tzotzil). This collective heart seeks common good; it serves as the epistemic and ontological core of political-ethical actions that "defines another paradigm of thinking and knowledge construction" (Barbosa 2019a), one rooted in everyday relationships with community, land, and territory (Mora 2017). An example of the importance and centrality of the heart can be heard in

6 *Comunalidad* describes a Mesoamerican Indigenous collectivism in which the social life of peoples is defined and articulated by their interrelationship with their land and territory. Anthropologist Benjamín Maldonado has written about comunalidad in the context of the Indigenous peoples of Oaxaca.

7 Orlando Fals Borda (2007) explains in an interview with Tomas Rodriguez Villasante the origin of the concept *sentipensante*. It arises from the amphibious life described in his "*Historia doble de la Costa*" where a fisherman who accompanied him in the swamps said, "We believe that we act with our heart, but we also use our head, and when we combine the two things; we are *sentipensantes.*"

8 Grounded in the philosophy of her Tseltal language, Pérez Moreno (2021: 74) describes how the heart (*o'tan/o'tanil*) is a way of being-feeling-thinking-saying-doing-living that encompasses a range of emotions, feelings, thoughts, and actions of all beings that inhabit the cosmos.

Zapatista discourse as well as in the common quotidian greeting "How is your heart?" or by asking, "What does your heart tell you?" when faced with important decisions.

Everything for everyone

Recognizing our part in a terrestrial community, the ethos of a Zapatista Seed Pedagogics promotes a deeply respectful, as well as conjoined, dignified humility that moves towards the horizon of what in Tseltal and Tzotzil languages is called *lekil kuxlejal*[9]—a utopia of good living/existing for all beings on the planet. Its daily practice resists the normalization of oppressive conditions. Beyond mere survival, this horizon of Zapatista Seed Pedagogics is the vital evolution of the diverse and embodied memory of any seed; a celebration of the full potential of life itself. This attention to vitality pervades everyday actions in the reproduction and care of all aspects of living: from caring for home, planting and harvesting, in all social and political spheres, where all beings are honored. Derived from Mayan and other Mesoamerican cosmologies syncretized with liberatory currents of Catholicism, this spiritual core manifests in the many evolving rituals that accompany the flow of seasons, celebrations, production of food and medicine, rites of passage through stages of life, as well as reconnection with, and defense of, the territory. The traditional Mayan fire ceremony is just one example of honoring the dead or celebrating an accomplishment, such as that carried out at Acteal in remembrance of the 1997 massacre. Another example is seen in the crosses one sees placed at water springs, sometimes named after a Catholic saint, marking a holy site that predates colonialism, with previous names to that of the current syncretic festive day of ritual celebration.

Territorialized roots

Zapatista Seed Pedagogics are rooted in the territories from which they emerge, whose peoples' languages express deeply communal ideas and practices. Like many other contemporary Indigenous peoples in

9 In the Tzotzil and Tseltal Mayan languages.

Mesoamerica, the Tzotzil, Tseltal, Tojolabal, and Ch'ol communities of the Zapatista movement still live close to the land (Lenkersdorf 2008), collectively tending a *milpa*[10]of crops, as well as the milpa of their community. Although these various linguistic groups are all Mayan peoples, there are differences in their histories and expressions—social memories and philosophies diverge even among people of the same ethnicity—as well as frictions among them. Zapatismo as a political-ethical expression has evolved from these diverse communities' common ancestral ways of knowing, being and doing, as well as through interactions with outside influences.

Learning while walking

An example from Tseltal pedagogical philosophy can help reveal the significance of the collective *milpa*, as both sustenance and education. Juan López Intzín (2015) describes the *milpa* as a pedagogy itself. He refers to the milpa both as location (the food forest, garden, or fields containing an intricate ecology of multispecies participation in the production of mutual nourishment), as well as a place and mechanism of learning and production. He describes the milpa as a "walking [while] learning to live" in a communal way with all beings. Literally and metaphorically, Intzín highlights the value of each grain as vital to community life. Each seed signifies a human intervention in a long history of interspecies co-evolution. Each member of the community "learns to gather-collect [as] knowledge and the simultaneous teaching-learning about life in the field. All seeds are gathered and require *kanantayel* (care) because the subsistence and continuity of family and community life depends on it," (Intzín 2015: 79). Intzín highlights the contribution of each being/element towards the common good through territorially derived language that describes ways of knowing, being, and doing in close interrelation with their natural environment and daily praxis. Those of us who attended *Escuelita*, the Zapatista Little School, came to experience this *caminando*

10 The Spanish word *milpa* is derived from the Nahuatl word *milli-pan*, which describes the continental ancestral technology of planting corn, squash, beans, and other endemic plants together in such way that they support each other both structurally and chemically: bean vines crawl up the corn stalk while fixing nitrogen in the soil; squash vines spread horizontally and shade the soil. *La milpa* is an ancient technology of basic sustenance that carries cultural identity and knowledge.

aprendiendo, this "learning while walking" pedagogy in the daily collective work and home life we shared with Zapatista families during that week.

Interrelated life: *mandar obedeciendo*, leading by obeying

This Zapatista principle of *mandar obedeciendo*[11] (leading by obeying) is central to Zapatista Seed Pedagogics and also perhaps the most difficult to understand from a modernist episteme. It has an even deeper significance on an ecosystemic level, as it gestures towards a commonality of intertwined life for all beings and elements that depend on each other. To lead by obeying alludes both to ways of human governance and politics, as well as to an environmental epistemology (Leff 2006) that sees humans as part of nature. Thus, leading by obeying is in the service of everything for everyone, or *todo para todos* as an oft-repeated Zapatista maxim of equity declares, mirroring a relationship of communality that extends beyond the human. This manifests in festivities and rituals around planting, caring, and harvesting that are carried out in conjunction with the seasons, climate, elements, and community needs. These do not revolve around capitalist calendars or profit exigencies, nor is it an individual decision, but rather a communal process of learning and teaching with close listening to each other, the land, plants, animals, and elements that follows the principle of *mandar obedeciendo*.

The *caracol* as a spiral in/out of each other's hearts

Zapatista Seed Pedagogics teach and practice interbeing and interdependence with community—including the natural world and cosmos—stretching from microscopic to vast scales. This is often represented through the image and motion of a spiral conch shell, a *caracol* such as those of snails and other mollusks. The spiral of this caracol is a "paradigm of symbolic thought for Mayan peoples," wrote historian Andres Aubry, where "caracol is a concept that transcends and encircles the words used to describe it" (Aubry 2003). Images of caracoles abound

11 *Mandar obedeciendo* is one of the most important Zapatista principles that reflects their assembly-based decision-making process for the common good, as well as the authorities' mandate to carry out the common good of the people.

in Mesoamerican pre-Columbian codexes representing speech, and are constantly recreated in Zapatista embroidery, murals, books, and paintings. It is a common practice to blow a conch shell to call a community to assembly or ritual. This potent cultural and historical symbolism is recreated geographically in Zapatista autonomous territory where autonomous administrative zones are called caracoles, each bearing its own descriptive name.[12] According to Barbosa:

> The denomination of Zapatista territory using the word caracol is linked to a cyclical conception of time as opposed to the linear vision of history. A caracol is also an instrument used to call the community to assembly, an invitation to collective dialogue and active participation of each person in communal life. Ancestrally, it represents coming out of one's interiority to enter the heart of the other, in dialogic communication with a spiral path, in continuous endogenous and exogenous movement. In the same way, it represents the slow pace of the snail, which symbolizes the construction process of communication, dialogue, and debate amongst Zapatista communities [that continues] until a consensus is reached (2019c: 92 93).

The multifaceted symbolism of the caracoles also applies to the extension and hospitality of the Zapatista movement.[13] Good Government Councils at each administrative caracol receive outsiders who come to Zapatista territory for different reasons: perhaps to partake of their autonomous health or justice systems (as these are also open to non-Zapatistas), or because they feel compelled to learn more about the movement's process of building autonomy and their ethical-political approach. As Barbosa points out, the snail's slow pace illustrates the participatory process of inclusion as well as being a counterpoint to speed.

---

12 A few examples: Caracol La Realidad is "Mother of the Caracoles, of the Sea of our Dreams;" Caracol Oventic is "Resistance and Rebellion for Humanity;" Caracol Morelia is "Whirlpool of Our Words."

13 Mendoza and García (2015) explain how, for the Zapatistas, the caracol represents "entering the heart (knowledge), in turn leaving the heart to walk in the world (life), so there is a movement back and forth..."

Affirming life

A Zapatista Seed Pedagogics' self-reflexive methodology, broad spatial-temporal reach, and complex spiral motions across different scales are all educational components needed in today's global social movements. Multiple forms of resistance are necessary to counteract the intensifying violence wrought by an ongoing colonial-capitalist project of unfinished conquest. Since their 1994 uprising, the Zapatistas demonstrated the enormous failure of nation-states to ensure basic conditions of dignified life for Indigenous peoples. In their First Declaration of the Lacandon Jungle,[14] they outline basic demands to land, housing, food, health, education, work, independence, freedom, democracy, justice, and peace. These life-affirming rights are inherent to the Zapatista ethical-political-educational struggle and denied by a capitalism that seeks to separate, absorb, or annihilate anyone who resists. In individualist societies, the challenge is to resist collectively. Zapatista Seed Pedagogics builds a collective political-ethical consciousness, through a decolonizing educational process of intersubjective encounter and exchange occurring across geographies. This carries great potential for creating a collective revolutionary subject globally in a time when it is most needed for the survival of the planet (Barkin and Sánchez 2019).

A long historical memory

Remembering and reconnecting to ancestral ways of knowing and being is crucial to a re-existence[15] of Indigenous peoples as survivors of genocide who still confront ongoing neocolonial projects of extraction and extermination. These ancestral ways include recognizing human

14 Since 1994, the Zapatista movement has issued six declarations of the Lacandon Jungle, in addition to a wide range of political communiqués. You may find them archived at http://enlaceZapatista.ezln.org.mx

15 The term *rexistencia* emerges from diverse Mesoamerican experiences involving the defense of land and territory by Indigenous/original peoples who continue to resist even when faced with ongoing attempts to exterminate or conquer them. The term is also apropos in processes of decolonization as Indigenous people constantly reinvent themselves given the "Modernity" they must deal with. It also refers to the emergence of movements that are consciously returning to traditional, previously subjugated forms and practices. *Rexistencia* is similar to what Nishnaabeg scholar Leanne Betasamosake Simpson (2017) terms "Indigenous resurgence"

interconnection and relationality (Escobar 2012) with all earthly beings and elements like other animals, plants,[16] fungi, insects, soils, microbes, forests, mountains, rivers, rocks, clouds, rains, and winds. The confluence of resources within a common terrestrial history are meant to be shared and contributed to. This understanding runs counter to the modern ideal of human superiority as well as to that of capitalist domination by acknowledging these all as beings with as much dignity and worth of respect as persons. This respect is crucial for a balanced coexistence with the web of relationships that confer life on earth. Zapatismo politicizes this understanding, which forms the ethical ground of its Seed Pedagogics with the conviction that a dignified and just human existence is only made possible by engaging respectfully with all other terrestrial beings.

Building true communication

Through their inherited linguistic structures and concepts, Zapatistas embody and enact these values. For example, the equivalent of "we" is frequently heard in Maya languages of Chiapas, expressed in Tseltal and Tzotzil by the suffix *tik*. This repeated suffix highlights a way of knowing, being, and doing that is shared and in relation. This concept of "we/us" is inherent to the languages' structure (Lenkersdorf 2008), often describing relationship with other human and environmental entities. Tseltal, Tzotzil, and Tojolabal all contain intersubjective relationship in their structure. In this way, these languages' words and structures embody the shared space of careful listening as well as heartful speaking that are necessary to come to full and common understanding. This reveals the cultural importance of knowing how to listen to another, and the importance of building a "we" through dialogic exchange where the participation of each subject is essential, coming from their own autonomy, knowledge, and perspective.

Carlos Lenkersdorf (2008) gives us an example of this intersubjectivity with his explanation of the form, "I speak; you listen," rather than the subject-object construction of "I tell you." Each subject puts their attention and intention towards opening and expanding themselves to

16 The work of Canadian forest ecologist Suzanne Simard (1997) who studies the communication and social life of trees, has revealed that trees and humans share 50% of their DNA.

gain a deeper understanding of the other; both subjects collaborate and reach outside of themselves. It requires each subject to value the other as equal, in common intention towards a truly shared communication. Looking and listening with full and deep attention develops a practice of opening one's consciousness and senses to be able to look and listen to alterity with dignity and respect. Lenkersdorf points out how "listening" is both a disposition and capacity to listen beyond oneself; a listening not only in dialogue with another, but a listening that allows the "we" to be constructed, the *ke 'ntik*:

> In the "we" of Maya Tojolabal, the "I" is not denied, but is integrated into the "we" through commitment. Thus, through the commitment of the particular "I's" that are listened to, the "we" is integrated. All the members of the "we" form a single body, in which each one is respected and listened to, and in which all have a part in decision making (Ariño and Fernández 2012: 293 298).

This linguistic structure expresses the concepts reflected in their social relations. What does it mean to learn-teach within this conception of the *tik*? Lenkersdorf (2008) recounts an anecdote of how his Tojolabal students took an exam collectively: they consulted one another to solve their questions, each person participating in the collective exam-taking. This was not about individual competition, but rather about working on the problems together; the presence and participation of each person is necessary to construct a "we" and a shared knowledge.

The liberatory role of memory

Such collective learning-teaching practices were revived and reformulated in the liberation theology of Bishop Samuel Ruiz, whose diocese made an important contribution to the consciousness-raising that would lead to the Zapatista mobilization. Beginning in the 1960s, Ruiz promoted a liberatory interpretation of God's word that helped many Indigenous people discover themselves as humans worthy of equal and respectful treatment. Collective memory of the racist injustices endured by multiple generations on large landholdings in Chiapas, emerges in Mariana

Mora's Indigenous testimonies. These narrate a "process of conscious and constant reflection in [collectively] rethinking history and historicity" (Mora 2017: 79).

Together, these testimonies reveal an aspect of Zapatista Seed Pedagogics; they demonstrate how a collective body working for common good draws on multiple perspectives enabling a larger, and more complete, historical memory. In assembly, this allows for a more complex discussion that can lead to more shared agreement. Listening, speaking, and acting for collective benefit does not emerge from lengthy individual reflection, says Lenkersdorf; rather it is the result of a long history and generations of experience.

Awakening and building a collective heart

Necessary for a liberatory education is what Paolo Freire (1970) would call *conscientizaciaõ*,[17] where each person comes to contextualize their relationship to the world through a process of articulating their experience.[18] Awakening a critical consciousness of being with and in the world (Freire 1970; Barbosa 2015) begins a journey of epistemic decolonization that brings an emphasis to ethical relationship in liberatory education (Dussel 2019). This implies a relationship of equals, in recognizing each subject as not only as innately worthy as a being, but also carrying worthy knowledge and experience.

Similarly, Intzín (2015) refers to a cultural and historical process of collective reflection that enables decisions to be made through a consideration of everyone's perspective. He draws connections between ancestral Mayan knowledges, and the ideas and methodologies still practiced in everyday life, such as community assemblies for decision-making. In his explanation of the term *ch'ulel*,[19] Intzín describes a process

17 *Conscientizaciaõ* is the original Portuguese word to describe political-educational aware-ness-building, a process of raising consciousness of one's value, power, and structural relation-ship to the world.

18 In his 1997 talk at Lesley college shortly before he died, Freire spoke of the necessary interrelationship between action and reflection in learning and teaching for a liberatory education (field notes, Sáenz).

19 *Ch'ulel* is often translated into Spanish as, *alma/corazón*, or soul/heart in English.

not unlike Freire's conscientizaciõ, nurtured through the "acquisition and development of word, speech, and consciousness." In opening our eyes to the contradictions of our material reality, taught Freire, we can come to a deeper knowledge of it, by way of respectfully seeing and listening to others. Doing this encourages us to evaluate our conditions and practices, to discern what benefits us together, what does not, and what we need to change. From the fields of education and philosophy, both Freire (1970) and Intzín (2015) describe a pedagogical process involving a congruency of *palabra verdadera* (true word) with everyday actions, with similar methodologies of deep engagement that encourage us to develop discernment as both individual and collective subjects.

Learning to listen

In the Mayan languages discussed, *la escucha* (a deep listening to the heart of the other) is crucial for establishing an intersubjective relationship with mutual understanding. It is essential for building together while respecting our differences, a mutual reach, without any one subject overpowering the others. *Detrás de nosotros estamos ustedes*,[20] says a Zapatista slogan that maintains the difference of subjects without subjugating any of them (Sáenz 2008); it is an "I am you" or "we are you-all" construction that maintains the union of equals without losing difference. To truly listen, one needs to practice radical hospitality to the other, open oneself up to both give and receive, without any obligation, subjugation, or hierarchy. This ability to respect differences while maintaining integrity builds communality. As Lenkersdorf writes:

> Receiving holds a secret: it is the other, it is the others whose words we do not create, whose words are not the product of our actions, but come from outside and take us out of the center where our self prefers to be   in order to command, direct, and be on top. Taking ourselves out of the center does not marginalize or push us towards the periphery, but rather integrates our I into the we (2008: 18).

20 This phrase is almost impossible to translate satisfactorily into English as it contains a paradoxical use of plural terms for self and other. A literal translation is "Behind Us We Are You All."

Lenkersdorf describes this deep kind of listening as a "cosmoaudition," with the ability to transport us to other realities, as different worldviews tend to do. A horizontal interlocution is realized through looking and listening with focused attention and open sensitivity. It is the kind of close attention that a scientist or an artist gives to their subject or interlocutor. Yet only when realized respectfully, intersubjectively, not from a lens of superiority, can a more communal, non-hierarchical perception and understanding emerge, a depth often invisible to a modernist episteme. Lenkersdorf and Intzín describe this type of interlocution as one not limited to communication only with other humans, but rather one that extends to communication with all of creation: animals, plants, mountains, rivers, fire, humidity, and even the dead. Everything has inherent value and communicates in its own way.

Listening with the heart is more than an approach to another person; it responds to a need for completeness that allows us to come out of our inner self, to stop being alone with only one of us. The way we come to know this world is filtered through what we are open enough to see, perceive, feel, and be. Our perception can be expanded or restricted by will and by the limits of our consciousness, experience, and/or imagination. Barbosa describes how for the Zapatistas "the heart remains the epistemic and ontological core of their feelings, their words, their thinking, and their political action, signaling another paradigm of thinking and for building knowledge" (2019b: 31). Barbosa writes,

> the unity between body soul reason feeling, dimensions of human existence dissociated by modern western science, is recovered. This unity is present in the historical path of political resistance of many Indigenous peoples, peasants, riverside dwellers, and quilombolas, among other peoples of the countryside, waters, and forests throughout Latin America. It is a journey triangulated between fire and word, between contexts of war for (re)existence and with a voice located in a thought, which is also feeling, since it is at one in the heart (Barbosa, 2019b: 32 33).

In Zapatista Seed Pedagogics, the collective heart is empowered by a mutual learning-teaching process across geographies and time, a spiral of historical and cultural memory reaching into each heart that yearns for liberatory connection and a good life in common. It spirals out globally in the form of an emerging political, and potentially revolutionary, collective subject who together is building *un mundo donde quepan muchos mundos*, a world where many worlds fit, a world in which every being can thrive.

References

Aubry, Andrés. "Los Caracoles Zapatistas." *La Jornada*, November 2003.

Barbosa, Lia Pinhero. "Paradigma Epistêmico do Campo e a Construção do Conhecimento na Perspectiva dos Movimentos Indígenas e Camponeses da América Latina." In *Educação e Movimentos Sociais: Análises e Desafios, Volume 4*, edited by Arlete Ramos de Santos, Livia Andrade Coelho, and Julia Maria da Silva Oliveira. Brazil: Paco Editorial, 2019a.

. "Estética da Resistência: Arte Sentipensante e Educação na Práxis Política Indígena e Camponesa Latino Americana." *Conhecer: Debate Entre o Público e o Privado* 9, no. 23 (2019b): 29 62.

. "O Popol Wuj na Contemporânea Luta Indígena Mesoamericana," *Tensões Mundiais* 15, no. 28 (2019c): 75 102.

. *Educación, Resistencia y Movimientos Sociales: La Praxis Educativo Política de los Sin Tierra y de los Zapatistas*. Mexico City: UNAM, 2015.

Barkin, David and Alejandra Sánchez. "The Communitarian Revolutionary Subject: New Forms of Social Transformation," *Third World Quarterly* 41, no. 8 (2020): 1421 1441.

Dussel, Enrique. *Pedagogics of Liberation: A Latin American Philosophy of Education*. Trans. by David I. Backer and Cecilia Diego. Goleta, CA: Punctum Books, 2019.

Escobar, Arturo. "Cultura y Diferencia: La Ontología Política del Campo de Cultura y Desarrollo," *Wale'keru: Revista de Investigación en Cultural y Desarrollo* 2 (2012): 7 16.

Fals Borda, O. "Orlando Fals Borda Concepto Sentipensante," interview by

Tomas Rodriguez Villasante, October 9, 2017, video https://www.youtube.com/watch?v mGAy6Pw4qAw.

Freire, Paolo. *Pedagogy of the Oppressed, 30th Anniversary Edition*, trans. Bergman Ramos, M. (New York: Continuum): 2000 [1970].

Leff, Enrique. *Aventuras de la Epistemología Ambiental: De la Articulación de Ciencias al Ciálogo de Saberes*. Mexico: Siglo XXI Editores, 2006.

Lenkersdorf, Carlos. *Aprender a Escuchar: Enseñanzas Maya Tojolabales*. Mexico: Plaza y Valdés Editores, 2008.

López Intzín, Juan. "Ich'el Ta Muk': La Trama en la Construcción del Lekil kuxlejal. Hacia Una Hermeneusis Intercultural o Visibilización de Saberes desde la Matricialidad del Sentipensar Sentisaber Tseltal." In *Prácticas Otras de Conocimiento(s): Entre Crisis, Entre Guerras. Tomo I*, edited by Xochitl Leyva et al. CLASCO, 2015.

. "Ich'el ta muk': La Trama en la Construcción del Lekil kuxlejal (Vida Plena Digna Justa). In *Senti pensar el Género: Perspectivas desde los Pueblos Originarios*, edited by Georgina Méndez Torres et al. Editorial La Casa del Mago, 2013.

Maldonado Alvarado, Benjamín. "La Comunalidad Como Una Perspectiva Antropológica India." In *La Comunalidad: Modo de Vida en los Pueblos Indios*, edited by Juan José Rendón Monzón. Conaculta, México, 2003.

Mendoza Sánchez, Citlali and Raúl Ernesto García Rodríguez. "Discursos Ético Políticos y Prácticas Sociales Cotidianas en las Comunidades Zapatistas." In *Psicologia & Sociedade 27*, no. 3 (2015): 650 659.

Mora, Mariana. *Kuxlejal Politics: Indigenous Autonomies, Race, and Decolonizing Research in Zapatista Communities*. Austin: University of Texas Press, 2017.

Pérez Moreno, María Patricia.. "El Bats'il K'op Tseltal Frente al Proceso Colonial." In *Revista de la Universidad de México*, no. 3 (April 2021): 73 80.

Sáenz Boldt, Charlotte Marie, Lia Pinhero Barbosa, and Tania Cruz Salazar. "Pedagógica de Semilla en el Movimiento Zapatista: Siembra y Crecimiento de un Sujeto Colectivo Político." In *Revista PRÁXIS Educacional 17*, no. 46 (2021): 1 24.

Sáenz, Charlotte. "Learning to We." In *Journal of Aesthetics & Protest 6* (2008).

Simpson, Leanne Betasamosake. *As We Have Always Done: Indigenous Freedom Through Radical Resistance*. Minneapolis: University of Minnesota Press, 2017.

Wallerstein, Immanuel. *The Modern World System: Capitalist Agriculture and the Origins of the European World Economy in the Sixteenth Century*. New York: Academic Press, 1974.

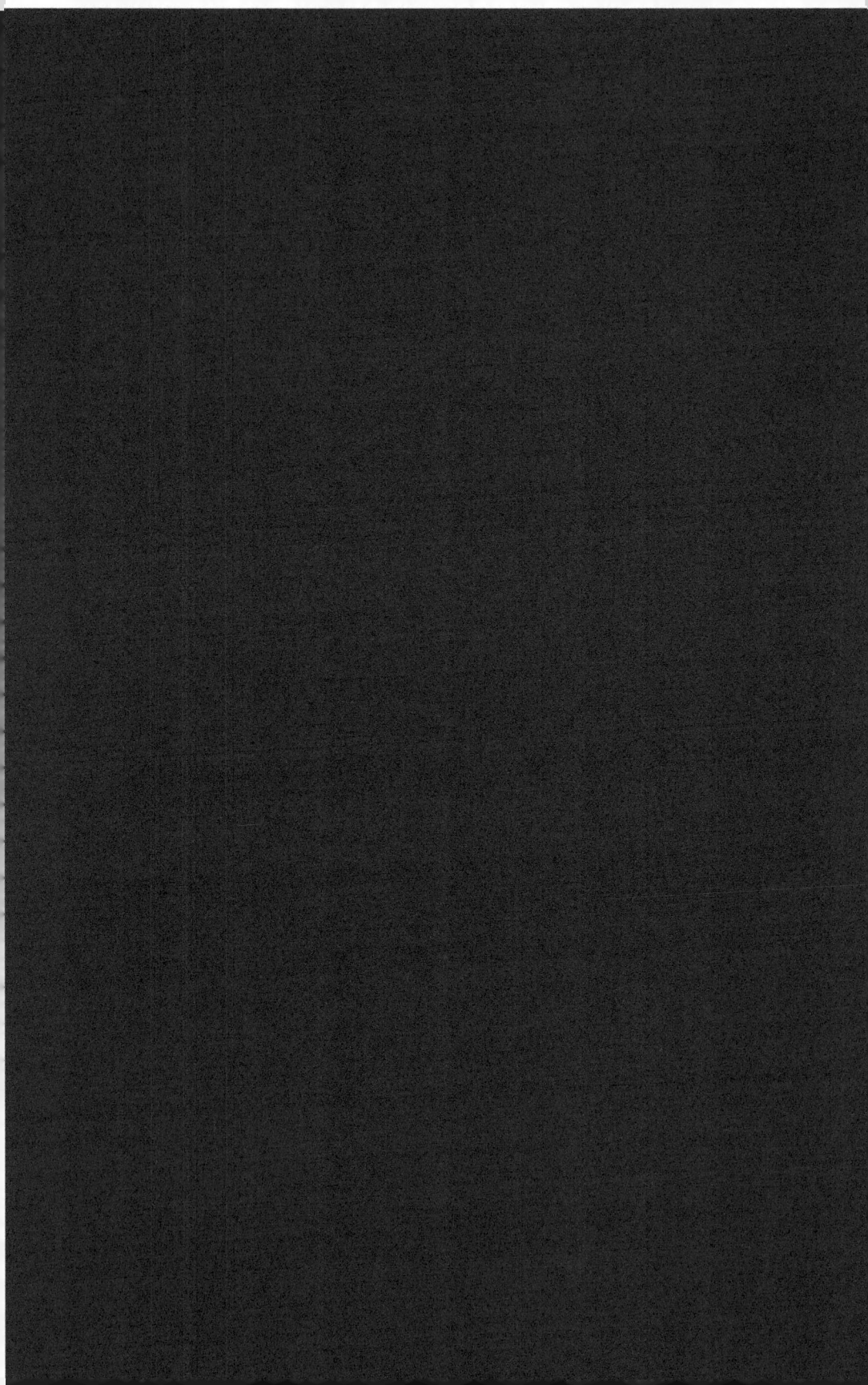

The Journey for Life
of the EZLN and CNI:
The Beginning

Rosa María Barajas and Enrique Davalos
Raíces sin Fronteras Collective

O n October 5, 2021, the Zapatistas surprised us with the
announcement that they would travel to the five continents,
beginning with Europe. As Subcomandante Insurgente Moisés
informed in a communiqué that day, "various delegations, men, women,
and others, the color of our earth, will go out into the world, walking or
setting sail to remote lands, oceans, and skies, not to seek out difference,
superiority, or offense, much less pity or apology, but to find what makes us
equal" (*see* "Part Six: A Mountain in the High Seas").

In the present article, we explore the circumstances, challenges, and
decisions taken by the Mayan Zapatista peoples to organize the first phase
of their "Journey for Life" in Europe. We will review their "Declaration for
Life" (2021) and other writings that explain the significance of the trip, as
well as the meaning given to the concept of "listening" as a form of struggle
and organization. We consider the complex obstacles and challenges
faced in the preparation of the journey and how the two delegations to

★ ★ ★

LISTENING AND SHARING THE WORD

The Zapatistas said they were going to Europe to listen. If we have learned anything from them, it is to listen with our ears and hearts wide open. In gatherings at the Caracoles with guests from outside, there are always Zapatistas from the communities taking notes, recording, listening, observing. In the women's gatherings, while those invited to Zapatista autonomous territory participate, sing, shout, and even compete to see who speaks loudest or expresses the most intelligent thought, the Zapatista women do not give their opinions, they do not judge, they only listen. Marijose from the 421st Squadron perplexed hundreds of women gathered at a meeting in Notre Dame des Landes, Nantes, France, when at the end, after listening to several speakers, she only said, "Thank you very much," when many present had been waiting for a great speech.

Silence can say more than a thousand words. The message can be implicit. "I listen to you, I respect your word, and I learn from it." Silence does not mean not listening, on the contrary, you can listen with your ears and with your heart. In the system of death we live in, we are losing our ability to listen, to really listen. We are taught to listen to our interlocutors without paying attention to their words, and if we do, it is only to prepare a response that is better, more intelligent, one that shows that we know more or that we have more or that we are better.

★ ★ ★

Europe were finally constituted: the maritime "421st Squadron" and the "Extemporaneous" airborne delegation. We will also see that the paramilitary aggressions against the autonomous Zapatista communities did not cease during the organization and development of the trip, and that the Zapatista initiatives in Mexico did not cease either, continuing the work of weaving networks and searching for partners in Europe in the defense of life.

Despite multiple difficulties and numerous obstacles, the Journey for Life was made possible thanks to the collective work that includes each and every one of the Zapatistas as well as the many people who have accompanied their steps from the outside over the years. When the trip was first announced, enthusiasm soared amid the ravages of the Covid-19 pandemic in Mexico and the world, and after a prolonged silence by the EZLN. Previously, the last communiqué to come out had been seven months earlier, in March 2020, when Subcomandante Insurgente Moisés explained that due to the pandemic, the Zapatista communities would close down and go on red alert (*see* "EZLN closes Caracoles Due to Coronavirus and Calls on People Not to Abandon Current Struggles"). The announcement of the trip was surprising, received with disbelief or joy by some, and with contempt by others. By April 2021, on the eve of their departure, more than a thousand groups from 30 European countries had invited the rebels to visit them and share the anti-capitalist struggles that they are waging there, many similar to those that Indigenous communities in Mexico are facing.

Between July and December 2021, two delegations with over 170 Zapatistas would travel through Europe, a land they renamed as *Slumil K'ajxemk'op* or "Rebellious Land," in Tzotzil. In two communiques in September 2021, SupGaleano reported that these delegations included five children (*see* "The Popcorn Commando Unit") and a women's soccer team (*see* "After 17. The Miliciana Ixchel-Ramona Division"). The delegations also included Marijose, a gender-queer person, Subcomandante Moisés, and Zapatistas from communities of Chol, Tzotzil, Tzeltal and Tojolobal languages, all of Mayan roots.

The airborne delegation, the Extemporaneous, was accompanied by 16 delegates from the National Indigenous Congress (CNI) and the

Indigenous Governing Council (CIG), headed by their spokesperson, María de Jesus Patricio Martinez, also known as "Marichuy." The CNI delegates represented the Mayan peoples of Yucatán, Campeche and Quintana Roo; the Popoluca from Veracruz; the Binnizá from Oaxaca; the Purépecha from Michoacán; the Rarámuri from Chihuahua; the Otomí from Mexico City; and the Nahua from Jalisco, Puebla, Michoacán, and Morelos. There were also delegates from the Front of Peoples in Defense of the Land and Water of Morelos, Puebla, and Tlaxcala, including Liliana Velazquez, the widow of Samir Flores Soberanes. Flores Soberanes had publicly challenged the construction of a gas pipeline and two thermoelectric plants a day before his murder in February 2019 (*see* "CNI/CIG/EZLN Denunciation of the Murder of Samir Flores Soberanes").

All members of the Journey for Life took with them their languages, their customs, their cosmovisions, and their stories of struggle and resistance against the racism, the paramilitaries, and the megaprojects such as the poorly named Maya Train, the Trans-isthmic corridor, the Morelos Comprehensive Project, and the mines, highways, and tourist complexes. They offered to share their word with their hosts, if they were invited to, but, first and foremost, they had come to listen. They set out on a Listen and Speak (*Escucha y Palabra*) Commission, putting the speaking after the listening to what those who had invited them want to share with them. Rather than engaging in large public and media events, they were interested in meetings where there could be an exchange of words.

The trip was symbolic. Twenty years before, in 2001, twenty-four delegates of the rebel army had toured 12 states in Mexico, from Chiapas to Mexico City, with the purpose of getting the government to recognize Indigenous rights and cultures, that is, to demand a place for the peoples in the Mexican nation. In a March 2021 opinion piece, "The March of the Color of the Earth" (*La Marcha del Color de la Tierra*), Mexican journalist Luis Hernández Navarro reflected on that march and quoted Subcomandante Marcos as having said, "On this journey, we Indigenous people have seen the map of national tragedy, from Chiapas to the Zócalo [the central square in Mexico City], the center of power, and we have been gaining a flower of Brown dignity."

In the October 5, 2020 communiqué, "Part Six: A Mountain on the High Seas," Subcomandante Insurgente Moisés said, writing on behalf of the Zapatista women, men and *otroas*,[1] "20 years later we will set sail and journey once again to tell the planet that in the world that we hold in our collective heart, there is room for everyone [*todas, todos, todoas*].[2] This is true for the simple reason that that world will only be possible if all of us struggle to build it."

The call for a Declaration for Life

With its announcement, mobilizations to make the trip possible began by the Zapatistas and adherents to their struggle in Mexico, the United States, and Europe. The journey had to become a reality; the Zapatista communities know how to keep their word, having shown that when they say they will do something, they will do it. The effort had to be huge and, as always, had to come from below and to the left.

On January 1, 2021, the 27th anniversary of the Zapatista armed uprising and in the midst of the pandemic, the EZLN published "Part One: A Declaration... for Life," the last in a series of six communiqués that began with the announcement of the trip. It was a call to unite all those who make rebellion for life and resistance for humanity their own:

> We are united by...
>
> The pains of the earth: violence against women; the persecution and contempt of those who are different in their affective, emotional, and sexual identity; the annihilation of children; genocide against the natives, racism, militarism, exploitation, dispossession; the destruction of nature.
>
> The understanding that a system is responsible for these pains. The executioner is an exploitative, patriarchal, pyramidal, racist, thief, and criminal system: capitalism.
>
> The knowledge that it is not possible to reform this system, educate it, attenuate it, file it down, domesticate it, humanize it.

1 *Otroas*: gender-queer term equivalent to "them"

2 *Todos*: all men, *todas*: all women, *todoas*: all gender-queer people

> The commitment to fight, everywhere and at all times   everyone
> in their own field   against this system until it is completely
> destroyed.

The Declaration was signed by thousands of organizations and individuals in dozens of countries and has since been translated into 19 languages.

Why did the Zapatista delegations go to Europe?

As in 1994, when despair reigned below and to the left in Mexico and the world, in 2020, when the pandemic plunged the world into fear, selfishness, and extreme individualism, the Mayan Zapatista peoples proposed that we open our hearts: "It is time for our hearts to dance again, and for their sounds and rhythm to not be those of mourning and resignation" (*see* "Part Six: A Mountain on the High Seas"). In the midst of the ravages of Covid-19, the EZLN proposed a journey through the five continents in search of what is the most common, profound, and vital to our existence: freedom. "We will go to find... the common dream that we share as a species, since, in Africa that seemed far away, we started walking from the lap of the first woman: the search for freedom that animated that first step... and that continues to walk" (*ibid.*).

Eight months later in another communiqué, "The Journey for Life: To What End?" SupGaleano elaborated on the goals of the trip. It was an invitation for all us to dialogue and exchange impressions about the state of the world. We well know that the Zapatista communities have been insisting there is a coming "storm" for years: that we are facing the imminence of an apocalyptic storm, the result and immediate logical consequence of the irrational actions of the "capitalist hydra," a system that, at the same time, is a multifaceted crime, a criminal mafia with a thousand heads that dominates the world, and a murderous machine that without judgment or feelings executes the crime.

The Zapatista peoples warn us that in its incessant and increasingly complex search for profit, the beast is leading us to the abyss. What is at stake is a good part of humanity, if not all of life and the planet itself. The dilemma, as seen by the Zapatista movement, is overwhelming: either we kill the capitalist beast or the beast will destroy us. That is why they were going to Europe: to dialogue. They were going, they said, "to confront our analysis and conclusions with the other that struggles and thinks critically." ("The Journey for Life: To What End?").

They sought dialogue, but not with just anyone. They wanted to talk with artists and scientists who also criticize capitalism, but above all they wanted to converse with peoples and communities that resist and rebel. Some of their fundamental questions: How do you see the storm? What can be done? What about you?

But they were also going to warm hearts. It is a "delusional" but "necessary" initiative; an unexpected and surprising step organized in the midst of this pandemic that is just a "prelude" to the "apocalypse;" it is a call that is not waiting for the pandemic to subside. "Mother Earth does not wait for the storm to pass in order to decide what to do, but rather begins to build long before", SupGaleano wrote in "Part Three: The Mission" (2020). He continued, "we are going... to thank the other for their existence... the teachings that their rebellion and their resistance have given us... To embrace the other and whisper in their ear that they are not alone... To whisper that resistance and struggle, the pain for those who are no longer here, the rage at the impunity of the criminal, the dream of an imperfect, but better world, a world without fear, are worth it." But "above all," SupGaleano elaborated, "we are going to look for accomplices... for life" (*see* "The Journey for Life: To What End?").

Facing and overcoming obstacles

> It was not easy. It has been tortuous, actually. To get to this point, we have had to face criticisms, advice, discouragement, calls for caution and moderation, open sabotage, lies, badmouthing, detailed accounts of difficulties, gossip, insolence, and a phrase repeated ad nauseam: "What you all are trying to do is very difficult, if not impossible" ("421st Squadron" 2021).

Throughout the planning and development of the trip, problems and situations arose that at times made it seem that it would not take place. Here, we mention some of them.

The ship. While the announcement of the trip was surprising, even more so was their plan to travel by ship. In various communiqués, including "Part three: The Mission," the EZLN showed how the delegates prepared, including how they built test ships. But it was not easy to find a real one, even less on a tight budget, until they found an almost a century-old German sailboat about to be retired called the *Stahlratte* ("Steel Rat"). In the May 2020 communiqué called "Dolphins!" SupGaleano announced that the crew agreed to transport the 421st Squadron, the first group that had just set sail from Isla Mujeres.

Covid-19. The pandemic wreaked havoc, causing delays. It had been estimated that April 2021 would be the time for a group of several hundred Zapatistas to travel, however the situation around the world was still critical at that time. The delegates chosen to travel were quarantined for months, away from their communities and families, causing some to drop out. Covid-19 vaccines had taken a long time to arrive in Chiapas. When they finally did, they were mostly CanSino or Sputnik, which are not recognized by the World Health Organization and therefore, did not meet the travel requirements of the governments of the old continent. The Zapatista delegation thus had to wait and search for where the accepted vaccines from Pfizer, AstraZeneca, or Sinovac were available. Some *compañeras* received their vaccination a few days before their departure. The borders to several countries were still closed, especially for countries considered "high risk," such as Mexico. The arrival of the seven members of the 421st squad to Vigo, Spain, was without incident. However, the airborne delegation that would arrive later by plane had to change their port of entry from Paris to Vienna because the French government did not grant the entry permit.

Racism. In addition to the pandemic, one of the greatest obstacles was racism: the same historical and contemporary, systemic, open, and veiled racism that has long surrounded the life of the Zapatista communities. This time, racism became more evident when the travelers tried to obtain their passports. In June 2021, SupGaleano addressed a letter to *Llegó la hora de los* *pueblos*, a coalition of artists, intellectuals, and scholars, where he narrated what they were going through:

> it turns out that our compañeras, compañeros, and compañeroas3 meet all of the demanded requisites, make the stipulated payment, travel from their communities to the offices of the badly named "Secretary of Exterior Relations" (SRE) and, despite the pandemic, make an appointment, wait in line and for their turn and...the document is denied to them. [...] Yes, all of those papers are presented, but the problem is that, in the eyes of the Secretary of External Relation's bureaucrat, the color of skin, the manner of speech, the way of dressing, and the place of origin are what matters. ("Letter from the Sixth Zapatista Comission to the Collective 'Llegó la hora de los pueblos'").

The complaint was multiplied by support groups in Mexico and in various parts of the world, forcing the Mexican government to pressure SRE bureaucrats to issue the passports the Zapatistas were entitled to from the beginning.

Racist obstacles multiplied on the other side of the Atlantic as well. The second part of the delegation, composed mostly of men that arrived in Spain on September 14th, lost their connection to Vienna due to excessive scrutiny and questioning from the Spanish immigration officers. As best they could, a new flight was arranged, and they finally joined the group that was already in Vienna. Months passed since the initial announcement and doubts caused by the complications grew.

The first delegation: the 421st Squadron

The day finally arrived. On April 10, 2021, Subcomandante Insurgente Moisés issued the communiqué "Journey to Europe..." where the Zapatistas announced that the first delegation, the maritime delegation, was ready. It was made up of four women: Lupita, Carolina, Ximena, and Yuli; two men:

---

3 *Compañero* (male) and *compañera* (female) and *compañeroa* (gender-queer) have no exact translation in English. They lie somewhere between "comrade" and "companion." In a political context, the term generally refers to someone who belongs to a particular organization or movement. For the CNI, CIG, and EZLN, *compa* is often used for short and refers to someone who they respect in the movement.

Bernal and Dario; and one they: Marijose, the "4-2-1" that would leave Isla Mujeres, Ixchel on May 3rd on the Steel Rat, which the delegation baptized as "the Mountain."

Why seven? Not because it had been planned that way. In fact, the idea had been for the entire delegation to travel by ship, but by then, most of them had not yet obtained their passports. The departure was pushed forward due to weather changes that the crew considered dangerous, and the Mountain left on May 2nd, as SupGaleano announced in "At Sea" (May 15, 2021).

After a journey of 50 days and nights through the Atlantic Ocean, passing through Cuba and the Azores Islands, the Mountain reached mainland European shores via the Port of Vigo in Galicia on June 20th:

> The European sky weeps with emotion. Its tears can't be distinguished from the ones that moisten the cheeks   weathered by sun, sea, anguish and adrenaline   of the intrepid 421st Squadron. In their step, their gaze, and their heartbeats, the Mayan people   the legend will say   crossed the Atlantic in 50 days and nights, in their long and turbulent journey for life ("We arrived", June 2021).

The first to disembark and make a statement was Marijose:

> In the name of the Zapatista women, children, men, elderly, and of course, others, I declare that from now on this place, currently referred to as "Europe" by those who live here, be called: Slumil K'ajxemk'op, which means "Rebellious Land" or "Land that does not give in nor give up." And that is how it will be known by its own people and by others for as long as there is at least someone here who does not surrender, sell out, or give up... ("The Landing" June 23, 2021).

The 421st Squadron stayed in Europe until September 10th. They participated in meetings in Spain and France in a reserved manner, listening, without speaking as instructed by the EZLN, awaiting the arrival of the Listening and Word Commission. On August 13, 2021, the 500th anniversary of the Fall of Tenochtitlán, in a truck dressed as a large ship, the Squadron led a parade that groups from Spain and various parts of Europe had been preparing for months. At the end of the parade, the Squadron took the floor:

> We have not come all this way to complain. Not even to denounce the bad government we have to put up with... today we are in front of you, but we are just the first wave of a much larger group. There will be up to 501 delegates. There are 501 of us just to show the bad governments that we are ahead of them. While they simulate a false celebration of 500 years, we (nosotros, nosotras, nosotroas) are already heading towards what is next: life...
>
> We see something, we hear something, we know something is happening and is going to happen.
>
> And that's why we are on this journey, because we think and know that we are not the only ones who struggle and we are not the only ones who see what is happening and is going to happen.
>
> Our corner of the world is a small geography of struggle for life.
>
> We are looking for other corners and we want to learn from them.
>
> That is why we came here, not to bring you reproaches, insults, claims, or to collect on unpaid debts ("Only 500 Years Later").

The 421st Squadron arrived back in Mexico City on September 11 full of impressions about Europe from below and what their stay in Slumil K'ajxemk'op was like. They also returned full of advice for the second delegation that was soon to leave for Europe.

The second delegation: the Extemporaneous, or the airborne company

The second Zapatista delegation had been ready for months. Listening ear ready? Popcorn Commando's toy cameras and shenanigans at the ready. The Ixchel Ramona with uniforms and balls ready for a soccer match they owed to Milan of Italy. Backpacks and Zapatista passports waiting on the table (*see* "The Zapatista Passport," June 2021). The movements in Europe, and especially Spain, were also ready and awaited them with great anticipation. According to the planned schedule, the airborne company had been scheduled to arrive before August 13. But by July, 62 of the 177 delegates did not yet have a Mexican passport, despite having complied with the requirements and payment, and after several visits to the Ministry of Foreign Relations offices. One of the arguments for rejecting their applications, in certain cases several times, was that their birth certificates, a necessary requirement to obtain a passport, were not processed at birth, but some time later. For the government, that kind of certificate is "extemporaneous," officially identified as having been issued after the first three years of life. They consider that those certificates are not sufficient proof of Mexican citizenship, especially in a state bordering Central America, a source of migration through Mexico to the United States. The Mayans had to prove that they were not from Guatemala or El Salvador. "The only thing left for them [the Ministry of Foreign Relations] to do is to ask the governments of Central America to say that we are not citizens of those countries," Subcomandante Insurgente Moisés wrote in a communiqué that July entitled "The Extemporaneous and a National Initiative."

In a country where it is common for children to be born not in hospitals but in homes in remote villages, hours from a city where there is a registry office, it is clear that the real reason for hindering the Zapatistas from obtaining passports is none other than outright racism, as SupGaleano asserted in the a letter sent to *Llegó la hora de los pueblos*, mentioned above. Due to this, the Zapatista delegation made the following resolution:

> As the Mexican State does not recognize our identity and
> origin, and tells us that we are "extemporaneous"... we
> have decided to baptize this unit of Listening and Word
> as "The Extemporaneous"... As we saw in the dictionaries,
> "extemporaneous" means "that it is inopportune, inconvenient,"
> or "that it is inappropriate for the time in which it happens."
> In other words, we are inopportune, inconvenient, and
> inappropriate.

Never before have we been so adequately defined. We are
happy that at last the Mexican state recognizes that this is how
it considers the original peoples of this geography called Mexico
("The Extemporaneous and a National Initiative").

It was only through pressure from intellectuals and activists that the
passports were finally obtained.

With passports in hand, the Extemporaneous left Chiapas for its
first stop, Mexico City, in a caravan of five buses and escorted by several
solidarity vehicles. It was the first time in several years that such a large
delegation of Zapatistas had left their autonomous communities. Their
departure caused a stir. It was no coincidence that their entire journey was
"accompanied" by the National Guard and state police patrols from each of
the states they passed through. The arrival at the shelter where they stayed
for a couple of days before leaving for Europe was very emotional, with
individuals and groups greeting them with cheers and various displays of
affection. Finally, on the morning of September 13, a group made up mostly
of women left the Mexico airport for Vienna. A second group, mostly men,
set out in the afternoon with the same destination.

Struggle and resistance in Mexico does not stop

The decision to plan and undertake the Journey for Life did not stop
despite a pandemic poorly managed by the authorities, and renewed,
ongoing paramilitary attacks. On the other hand, in the middle of planning,
the EZLN proposed a strategic political movement, an initiative in support
of the victims of murders, disappearances, and femicides.

A pandemic poorly managed by the state. The problems confronted
by the traveling delegation were part of the multiple challenges the
autonomous communities faced by the pandemic. Despite the closure of
the Zapatista communities in March 2020 due to the pandemic, in the
October 2020 communiqué announcing the trip, the EZLN revealed
that twelve of their *compañeros* had died from what seemed to have been
Covid-19. Having had no resources of their own or from the government
to do tests, they followed only the indications of trusted scientists who

recommended that they assume that any respiratory difficulty would be Covid-19. Like most Indigenous communities in the country, the Zapatista Mayan peoples have been marginalized and ignored by public and private health systems. There are not enough hospitals and the ones that exist do not have enough equipment or medicines. Among many inept governments in Mexico, Chiapas stands out for its slow and poorly managed vaccination campaign. On the other hand, the state government has arrogantly and falsely reported that its epidemiological traffic light is "green," that is, with a minimum number of infections, even as the population reports otherwise. As of November 2021, when this article was finalized, the Zapatista communities remained closed. They continued with strong hygiene measures and information campaigns, as well as the use of their traditional medicine to confront this unprecedented threat.

The pandemic has also affected their communities financially: coffee cooperatives suffered havoc when the commercial circulation chains in Mexico and the world shut down. And due to being closed to the public, the sale of their handicrafts is now limited.

Paramilitary attacks. A little over a month after the announcement of the trip, the attacks on the communities increased, leading some to speculate on whether it was coincidental. The attacks came especially by the ORCAO (Regional Organization of Coffee Growers of Ocosingo), a paramilitary group disguised as peasants, that the EZLN has been denouncing for years. On November 10, 2020, the Zapatista Good Government Council at New Dawn in Resistance and Rebellion for Life and Humanity published a denunciation reporting the kidnapping and torture of Felix Lopez Hernandez from Caracol Patria Nueva by the ORCAO. Three months earlier, this same group had looted and burned warehouses in the Moisés y Gandhi Autonomous Community, also part of the New Dawn in Resistance and Rebellion for Life and Humanity Zapatista Good Government Council, or Caracol 10. They denounced that the ORCAO shoots day and night against the community (Hernández Navarro, "Arde Chiapas," August 25, 2020).

On September 11, when the 421st Squadron was returning from Europe and the Extemporaneous was in quarantine and ready to leave from Mexico

City, the ORCAO kidnapped Sebastian Nuñez Perez and José Antonio Sanchez Juárez, authorities of the Good Government Council of the same autonomous zone, *Caracol Patria Nueva*. They were released eight days later. In the communiqué "Chiapas on the Verge of Civil War" published on September 19, when the Extemporaneous was already in Europe, the EZLN warned that the paramilitary group acts under the protection and with the complicity of the state governor, Rutilio Escandon. This character, the EZLN denounces, does everything possible to destabilize the state. The statement closes with a severe warning: "next time there won't be a communiqué. That is, there will no longer be words, but actions." In that same message, SupGaleano recognized that the liberation of his *compañeros* was achieved thanks to interventions of the Catholic Church and human rights organizations, as well as the mobilizations that took place in Mexico and other countries, but especially in Europe, already with members of the Extemporaneous. At the same time, the EZLN made a call to mobilize on the 24th of the same month at Mexican embassies and consulates, and at government offices in Chiapas. The demand was precise: that the politicians of that state "end their provocations and renounce their death cult." On the date proposed by the rebels, about one hundred demonstrations were held in various cities of Mexico and the world, mainly in Europe.

On November 21, the Ajmaq Network of Resistance and Rebellion located in San Cristóbal de las Casas, Chiapas, denounced a new armed attack of the Moises y Gandhi Zapatista Autonomous High School By ORCAO paramilitaries. For several hours they shot at the houses of community residents and ended by burning three classrooms at the school. According to the Ajmaq statement, in October the ORCAO had already threatened to attack the high school ("Ataque Armado Y Quema De La Secundaria Autónoma Zapatista De Moisés Y Gandhi Por Paramilitares De La Orcao").

A national initiative. It came as a great surprise that the EZLN called for participation in the "popular consultation" promoted and cunningly managed by the ruling party, MORENA. The *Morenistas* claimed that the survey was to determine whether the population wanted to prosecute former presidents for state crimes such as disappearances, murders, and femicides. But the question that the Mexican Supreme Court posed was different: rather than focusing on former presidents, it became, surprisingly, a judgment on the political system as a whole. The question was simple: whether or not something should be done to comply with the right to truth and justice of those who have been victims by actions and omissions of the Mexican state. The answer was also simple: yes. Who can say no to that right to truth and justice? That was the call of the Zapatistas: participate in the consultation with a yes. But not to leave it just there, rather to also to campaign for truth and justice. In July 2021, Subcomandante Insurgente Moises explained:

> We have to make a start, not by looking up, but by looking at the victims. We must turn the consultation into an "extemporaneous" consultation, in order to start, independent of those above, a movement for a Commission for Truth and Justice for the Victims, or whatever it may be called. Because there can be no life without truth and justice ("The Extemporaneous and a National Initiative").

Encounters in the Rebellious Land

Finally, the two groups of the Extemporaneous reached Europe, landing in Vienna, Austria. The first group, headed by Subcomandante Moisés, was greeted by dozens of people not only from Austria, but from various regions of Europe from below. In the heat of the day, at an event organized in front of the airport by their hosts, SubMoisés took the floor:

> We, Zapatistas women and men, original peoples of Mexico, are in Vienna. We come because we know that there are poor people, Indigenous peoples in other countries of the world and in cities ... We see the problem that capitalism has caused, which is the problem of life. Also of nature. Nature is going to end. That is what we have come to tell you. Do you not believe it? You are going to see it... We do not come to [talk to] large masses, we come to talk to those who want to talk to us and to those we want to listen to, to learn how they fight, how they think (Noriega 2021).

The Extemporaneous intensified the Zapatista invasion that the 421st Squadron had began. It was like a counter-conquest of Europe by Indigenous people with their native languages, their traditional costumes, and their decolonizing and rebellious thoughts; a counter-conquest of old Europe with its history of colonialism, empires, looting, palaces, and racism. After resting, the whole delegation met with European collectives to strategize how to reach the many places they were invited to. According to the words of Moises, they were divided into 28 groups of "Listening and Word" each formed by 5 to 6 individuals who immediately dispersed to reach various places simultaneously.

Together, Europeans and Zapatistas made maps dividing Rebellious Europe into zones. The first would be Germany, Scandinavia, Eastern Europe, and the Balkans, being mindful of the winter cold that could wreak havoc on Mexican delegations. Spain and Portugal, with less severe winters, were left for the final two months of 2021. One week later, the 16 CNI delegates joined the invasion. One of the first activities was their participation in a march against the destruction of nature in Vienna. At the end, a young woman, Libertad, took the floor and on behalf of the Zapatista communities made the crowd shudder with her words "There Is a Woman" (*see* the end of this essay for the full communiqué). For almost six months, the Zapatistas' steps in Slumil K'ajxemk'op sowed and spread the seed of the struggle for life and a world where many worlds can fit. First, it was the 421st Squadron, and later the Extemporaneous and the CNI delegates. They reached multiple corners in several countries among them: Austria, Finland, Holland, Germany, France, Ireland, Scotland, England, Italy, Denmark, Slovenia, Poland, Switzerland, and Spain. The Extemporaneous then returned to Mexico the first week of December.

Most of their encounters were private. They met with environmentalists, anti-patriarchal feminists, peasants, city workers, migrants, racialized people, victims of violence, women from the Kurdish and Palestinian diasporas, and with the Samis and other Indigenous peoples. They visited ecological farms, occupied places for housing, camps of movements against megaprojects, such as the Arctic train through the Sami peoples' territory, or the "Trans Adriatic" gas pipeline that would pass through Greece, Albania, and Italy, to mention a few. They shared how the exploitation of land and water in Mexico has its roots in European companies, such as the French Danone, owner of Bonafont, and the German Deutsche Bahn, a railway company with investments in the poorly named Maya Train project. Both corporations also build megaprojects in their own countries and are confronting groups that resist them. The Zapatistas met with old acquaintances, comrades who have followed their path since the beginning of the EZLN uprising, such as the collective ¡Ya Basta! from Milan, already familiar with Zapatista lands. They also dialogued and met new *compas*.

According to the initial announcement, Europe was the first chapter of the Journey for Life. The Zapatistas said they will go to the five continents, an expedition that reminds us of the 10-year-long night in which the EZLN prepared and organized the uprising of January 1st, 1994. Thus, this is only the beginning. What is missing is yet to come.

Stay tuned.

Steel Rat leaving Isla Mujeres, Mexico to Europe with the 421st Squadron.
Photo by Enrique Davalos.

The 421st Squadron: Bernal, Dario, Marijose, Ximena, Carolina, Lupita, Yuli.
Photo by Enlace Zapatista.

The Extemporaneous at the Mexico City airport leaving for Europe.
Photos by Rosa María Barajas

Popcorn Command. Photo by Enlace Zapatista.

Ixchel Ramona soccer team. Photo by Enlace Zapatista.

Demonstrations in Europe on September 24th demanding to stop aggressions against Zapatista communities

Map of the Journey for Life in Spain

Map of the Journey for Life in Italy

Map of the Journey for Life in Germany

Map of the Journey for Life in Wales, Ireland, Scotland, and England

GIRA ZAPATISTA VA A HOLANDA

Amsterdam - extemporary art, farming activities, land struggles, food waste

Eindhoven - Kurdish Women's movement, resistance

Amsterdam - Anarchism, struggles

Amsterdam - indigenous peoples, decolonization, indigenous struggles and resistance

Utrecht - migrant struggles, food autonomy, radical schools, unlearning toxic masculinity, slavery, resistance

Hague - art, poetry, struggles from the Global South, colonial and emancipatory history, human rights, democracy, gender equity

Amsterdam - resisting the Monarchy, land struggles

Amsterdam - Zapatista dialogues

Map of the Journey for Life in the Netherlands

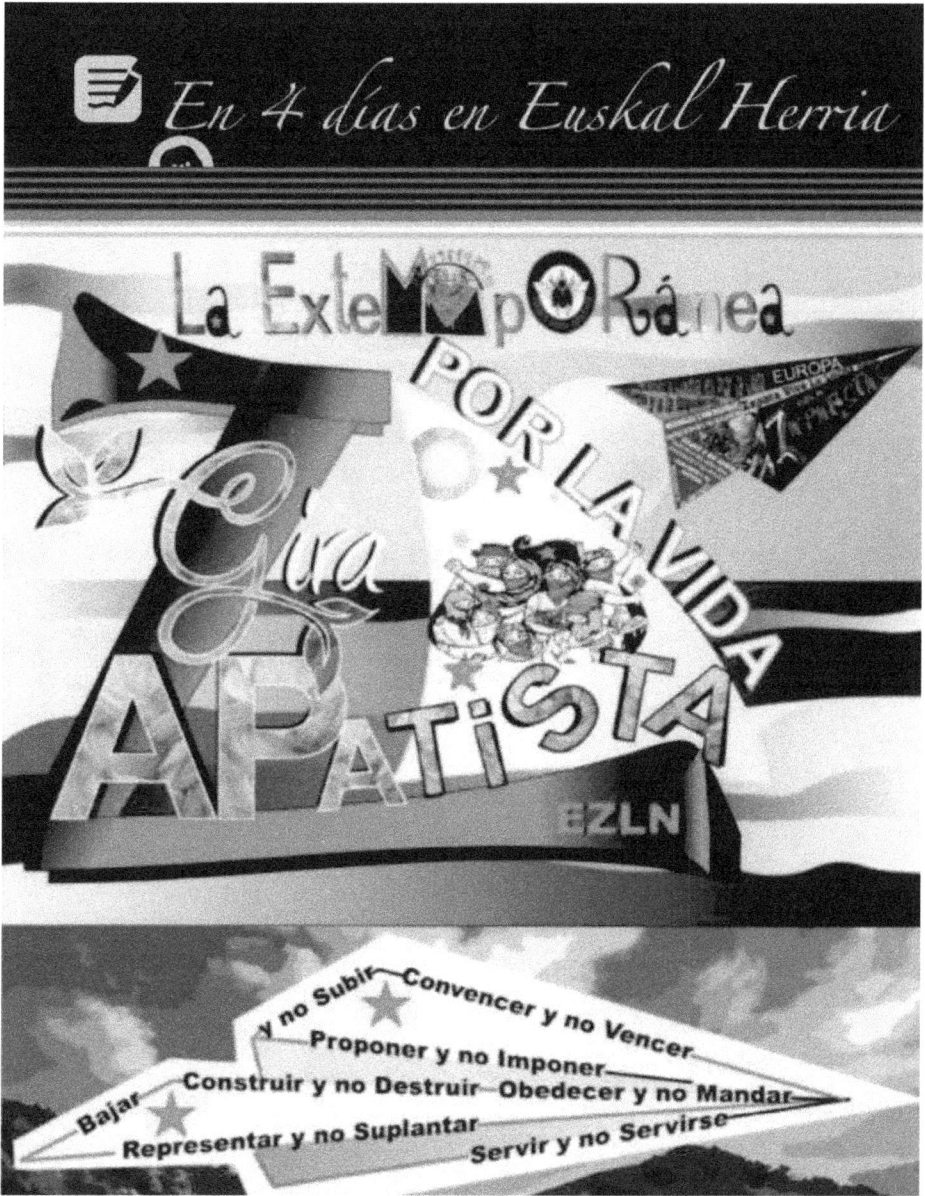

Map of the Journey for Life in Basque Country

THERE IS A WOMAN:
AGAINST THE DESTRUCTION OF NATURE.
VIENNA, AUSTRIA

WORDS OF THE ZAPATISTA COMMUNITIES
AT THE MARCH AGAINST THE DESTRUCTION OF NATURE
Vienna, Austria. In the voice of *compañera* Libertad, September 24, 2021.

Good afternoon.
These are our brief words in the form of a short story:

There is a woman.

The color of her skin does not matter, because she has all colors.

Her language does not matter, because she understands all languages.

Neither her race nor her culture matter, because all ways of being live in her.

Her size does not matter, because she is huge and nevertheless fits in one hand.

Every day and at all moments that woman is assaulted, beaten, wounded, raped, mocked and despised.

A male exerts his power over her.

*Every day and every hour, she comes to us [*nosotras, nosotros, nosotroas*].*

She shows us her wounds, her pain, her grief.

And we only give her words of consolation and pity.

Or we ignore her.

Perhaps as alms we give her something with which to treat her wounds.

But the man continues his violence.

We all know how this ends.

She will be murdered and with her death everything will die.

We can continue to give her only words of encouragement and medicine for her wounds.

Or we can tell her the truth: the only medicine that can cure her and heal her completely is for her to confront and destroy the one who is hurting her.

Knowing this, we too can unite with her and fight by her side.

We Zapatistas call that woman, "Mother Earth."

As for the man who oppresses and humiliates her, give him whatever name, face, or shape you want.

We, the Zapatista peoples, call that murderous man capitalism.

And we have arrived at these geographies to ask, to ask of you:

Are we going to go on thinking that we can treat today's blows with salve and painkillers, even though we know the wound will be bigger and deeper tomorrow?

Or are we going to fight alongside her?

We the Zapatista communities have decided to fight together with her and for her.

That is all we can say.

Thank you for listening to us.
Vienna, Austria, Europe, Planet Earth.
September 24, 2021.

Additional information

To learn more and to follow the Journey for Life, we recommend the following sources:

Enlace Zapatista
The EZLN page that publishes the Zapatistas' complete communiqués
http://enlacezapatista.ezln.org.mx

Bira Zapatista
"Ya Vienen," by Horazz and Suaiaren. September 21, 2021
https://www.youtube.com/channel/UCazRxQu9KyA_inkRoGBoVjw

Guilhotina.Info
https://guilhotina.info/en/2021/10/06/zapatistas firstdays europe

Radio Zapatista
https://radiozapatista.org

Radio Pozol
https://pozol.org

Camino al Andar
https://www.caminoalandar.org

Grieta.Org
http://www.grieta.org.mx/index.php/category/travesia por la vida

References

421st Squadron. "Only 500 Years Later." *Enlace Zapatista*, August 13, 2021. https://enlacezapatista.ezln.org.mx/2021/08/17/only 500 years later

Ajmaq Network of Resistance and Rebellion. "Ataque Armado Y Quema De La Secundaria Autónoma Zapatista De Moisés Y Gandhi Por Paramilitares De La Orcao." *Red Ajmaq*, November 21, 2021. English translation by Taller Ahuehuete and Schools for Chiapas, "ORCAO Armed Paramilitaries Attack And Burn the Zapatista Autonomous Middle School in Moisés and Gandhi." https://schoolsforchiapas.org/orcao attack and burn zapatista middle school

CNI CIG EZLN. "CNI/CIG/EZLN Denunciation of the Murder of Samir Flores Soberanes." *Enlace Zapatista*, February 20, 2019. https://enlacezapatista.ezln.org.mx/2019/02/21/cni cig ezln denunciation of the murder of samir flores soberanes/

Comandante Don Pablo Contreras and Subcomandante Insurgente Moisés "Part One: A Declaration... for Life." *Enlace Zapatista*, January 1, 2021. https://enlacezapatista.ezln.org.mx/2021/01/01/part one a declaration for life

Hernández Navarro, Luis. "La marcha del color de la tierra." *La Jornada*, March 2021. (Authors' translation.) https://www.jornada.com.mx/2021/03/16/opinion/012a2pol

. "Arde Chiapas." *La Jornada*, August 25, 2020. English translation by Chiapas Support Committee, "Chiapas Burns." https://chiapas support.org/2020/08/25/chiapas burns

New Dawn in Resistance and Rebellion for Life and Humanity Good Government Council. "Denunciation." *Enlace Zapatista*, Nov 12, 2020. http://enlacezapatista.ezln.org.mx/2020/11/12/denunciation from the new dawn in resistance and rebellion for life and humanity zapatista good government council new homeland caracol zapatista territory chiap

Noriega, Francisco with Independent Media in Vienna. "Account of the Zapatistas' arrival in Vienna and their first days in Europe." *Guilhotina*, October 6, 2021. https://guilhotina.info/en/2021/10/06/zapatistas firstdays europe

Subcomandante Insurgente Galeano. "Part Three: The Mission." *Enlace Zapatista*, December 22, 2020. https://enlacezapatista.ezln.org.mx/2020/12/24/part three the mission

. "421st Squadron." *Enlace Zapatista*, April 17, 2021.
http://enlacezapatista.ezln.org.mx/2021/04/20/421st squadron

. "At Sea." *Enlace Zapatista*, May 6, 2021.
https://enlacezapatista.ezln.org.mx/2021/05/15/at sea

. "Dolphins!" *Enlace Zapatista*, May 12, 2021.
https://enlacezapatista.ezln.org.mx/2021/05/17/dolphins

. "The Zapatista Passport." *Enlace Zapatista*, June 14, 2021.
https://enlacezapatista.ezln.org.mx/2021/06/19/the zapatista passport see you
soon portugal galicia here we come

. "Letter from the Sixth Zapatista Comission to the Collective 'Llegó la hora
de los pueblos'." *Camino al andar*, June 11, 2021.
https://www.caminoalandar.org/post/letter from the sixth zapatista comission
to the collective lleg%C3%B3 la hora de los pueblos

. "We Arrived." *Enlace Zapatista*, June 20, 2021.
https://enlacezapatista.ezln.org.mx/2021/06/22/we arrived

. "The Landing." *Enlace Zapatista*, June 23, 2021.
https://enlacezapatista.ezln.org.mx/2021/06/30/the landing

. "The Journey for Life: To What End?" *Enlace Zapatista*, June 27, 2021.
https://enlacezapatista.ezln.org.mx/2021/07/20/the journey for life to what end

. "After 17. (The Miliciana Ixchel Ramona Division)." *Enlace Zapatista*,
September 8, 2021.
https://enlacezapatista.ezln.org.mx/2021/09/12/after 17 the miliciana ixchel
ramona division

. "The Popcorn Commando Unit." *Enlace Zapatista*, September 10, 2021.
https://enlacezapatista.ezln.org.mx/2021/09/24/the popcorn commando unit

. "Chiapas on the Verge of Civil War." *Enlace Zapatista*, September 19, 2021.
https://enlacezapatista.ezln.org.mx/2021/09/20/chiapas on the verge of civil war

Subcomandante Insurgente Moisés. "EZLN closes Caracoles Due to Coronavirus and
Calls on People Not to Abandon Current Struggles." *Enlace Zapatista*, March 2020.
https://enlacezapatista.ezln.org.mx/2020/03/17/ezln closes caracoles due to

coronavirus and calls on people not to abandon current struggles

. "Part Six: A Mountain on the High Seas." *Enlace Zapatista*, October 5, 2020. http://enlacezapatista.ezln.org.mx/2020/10/07/part six a mountain on the high seas

. "Journey to Europe..." *Enlace Zapatista*, April 10, 2021. https://enlacezapatista.ezln.org.mx/2021/04/12/journey to europe

. "The Extemporaneous and a National Initiative." *Enlace Zapatista*, July 16, 2021. https://enlacezapatista.ezln.org.mx/2021/07/18/the extemporaneous and a national initiative

Zapatista communities. "There Is a Woman. Against the Destruction of Nature. Vienna, Austria." *Enlace Zapatista*, October 2, 2021. https://enlacezapatista.ezln.org.mx/2021/10/02/there is a woman against the destruction of nature vienna austria

www.ingramcontent.com/pod-product-compliance
Lightning Source LLC
Chambersburg PA
CBHW020457030426
42337CB00011B/137